CRAVING YOUR FAVORITE FAST FOOD BUT DON'T WANT TO SACRIFICE YOUR HEALTH? LOOK NO FURTHER!

Passionate home cook and social media star Karim Saad is here to prove that eating healthy doesn't have to be boring. *Exquisite Eats* offers a tasty selection of 85+ healthier, homemade versions of your go-to restaurant meals. Discover delightful recipes packed with flavor and nutrients so you can embrace the comfort and nostalgia of your favorite fast foods while staying committed to your health goals.

Designed for everyday use and equipped with meal plans and nutritional information, this cookbook uses easy methods to incorporate high-protein, balanced meals into a busy routine. You'll find breakfast recipes both sweet and savory to start your morning with; juicy burgers and fresh and spicy tacos for lunch; and hearty mains and satisfying desserts to cap it all off. No matter what you're in the mood for, there's something here for every meal of the day!

Exquisite!

EXQUISITE EATS

EXQUISITE EATS

85+ HEALTHY RECIPES
INSPIRED BY FAST-FOOD FAVORITES

——————

KARIM SAAD

Publisher Mike Sanders
Executive Editor Alexander Rigby
Editorial Director Ann Barton
Art & Design Director William Thomas
Designer Joanna Price
Photographer Ivan Solis
Food Stylist Adam Pearson
Recipe Tester Julie Lopez
Editorial Assistant Resham Anand
Developmental Editor Devon Fredericksen
Copy Editor Tiffany Taing
Proofreaders Mira S. Park, Lisa Starnes
Indexer Johnna VanHoose Dinse

First American Edition, 2025
Published in the United States by DK Publishing
1745 Broadway, 20th Floor, New York, NY 10019

The authorized representative in the EEA is Dorling Kindersley Verlag
GmbH. Arnulfstr. 124, 80636 Munich, Germany

Library of Congress Number: 2025930293
ISBN 978-0-5938-4261-4

DK books are available at special discounts when purchased
in bulk for sales promotions, premiums, fundraising, or educational
use. For details, contact SpecialSales@dk.com

Printed and bound in China

www.dk.com

MIX
Paper | Supporting
responsible forestry
FSC™ C018179

This book was made with Forest
Stewardship Council™ certified
paper – one small step in DK's
commitment to a sustainable future.
Learn more at
www.dk.com/uk/information/sustainability

To my parents: for your unimaginable
sacrifice and unshakable love.

And to my incredible community of over 6 million:
You've turned my passion into a platform,
and for that, I'll always be grateful.

CONTENTS

9 My Story
10 Why Duplicate Fast Food?
13 How to Use This Book
14 Essential Ingredients
15 Essential Tools
16 Sample Meal Plans
18 Sauce Cheat Sheet

BREAKFAST 21

23 Copycat Starbucks Kale & Mushroom Egg Bites
24 Copycat Starbucks Bacon & Gruyère Egg Bites
27 Hash Browns
28 4-Ingredient Protein Everything Bagel
31 Copycat Sausage & Egg McMuffin
32 Copycat McGriddle
35 Copycat Starbucks Spinach, Feta & Egg White Wrap
36 Copycat Philz Green Chile Burrito
39 Chocolate-Chip Baked Oats
40 Macro-Friendly Cinnamon-Roll Pancakes

STARTERS 43

45 High-Protein, Low-Calorie Garlic Cheese Bread
46 Loaded Bacon Cheddar Fries
49 Low-Calorie Poutine
52 Air-Fryer Mozzarella Sticks
55 Low-Calorie Tortilla Chips
56 High-Protein, Low-Calorie Loaded Nachos
59 Popcorn Shrimp
60 Chicken Nuggets
61 Healthier Bang Bang Chicken Bites
62 Chicken Tenders
65 Lemon-Pepper Wings
66 Garlic-Parmesan Wings
67 Buffalo Wings
68 Honey-Barbecue Wings

SIDES 71

73 Sweet Potato Fries with Low-Calorie Chipotle Aioli
74 Homemade Fast-Food Fries
77 Mexican-Inspired Loaded Baked Potato
78 Crispy Onion Rings
83 Healthier Caesar Salad with Yogurt Dressing
84 Crispy Smashed Potato Salad
87 Copycat Chick-Fil-A Southwest Salad with Creamy Salsa Dressing
89 Air-Fried Chips
90 Big Mac Salad
93 Chinese Takeout Fried Rice

HANDHELDS 95

97 High-Protein, Low-Calorie Grinder Sandwich
98 Healthier Copycat Popeyes Chicken Sandwich
101 Low-Calorie Copycat Chicken Snack Wrap
102 Healthier Copycat Chick-Fil-A Chicken Sandwich
103 Chicken Shawarma Wrap
105 Lower-Calorie California Burrito
106 Korean Beef Wraps
108 Grilled Kofta Pita Pockets with Tahini-Yogurt Sauce
109 Turkey Pesto Wrap

PIZZA 111

113 Keto Pizza Dough
114 Healthier Pizza Toasties
117 Easy Healthier Cheese Pizza
118 Barbecue Chicken Pizza with Lavash Bread

TACOS 121

123 Copycat Del Taco Chicken Soft Tacos
124 Crispy Buffalo-Chicken Tacos
127 Crispy, Baked Beef Tacos
128 Big Mac Smash Tacos
131 Chipotle-Shrimp Tacos with Creamy Slaw
132 Healthier Baja Fish Tacos

BURGERS 135

137 Turkey Burger with Lemon Aioli
138 Copycat Spicy McChicken Sandwich
141 Copycat McDonald's Cheeseburger
145 Copycat McDonald's Big Mac
146 Copycat Whopper
149 Healthier Copycat Juicy Lucy Burger
150 Healthier Copycat In-N-Out Double-Double
153 Healthier Steakhouse Burger

MAINS 155

157 Healthier Chicken Parmesan
160 Healthier Copycat Panda Express Orange Chicken
162 Copycat Panda Express Teriyaki Chicken
163 One-Pan Lemon-Chicken Orzo Pasta
165 One-Pan Korean Fried Chicken
166 Honey-Chipotle Chicken Rice Bowl
169 High-Protein Mac 'n' Cheese
170 Honey-Barbecue Slow-Cooker Meatballs
173 Healthier One-Pot Lasagna Bowl
174 Firecracker Salmon Bites
177 Healthier Fish & Chips

SWEETS 179

181 Healthier Rice-Cake S'mores
182 Healthier Moist Chocolate Cupcakes
185 Strawberry Cheesecake Cups
186 Oreo Protein Cheesecake Cups
189 Healthy Oat-Flour Carrot Cake
192 Healthier Air-Fried Glazed Donuts
195 Protein Copycat Cinnabon Rolls
196 Japanese Soufflé Pancakes
199 Healthier Milkshakes

201 Acknowledgments
202 Index
208 About the Author

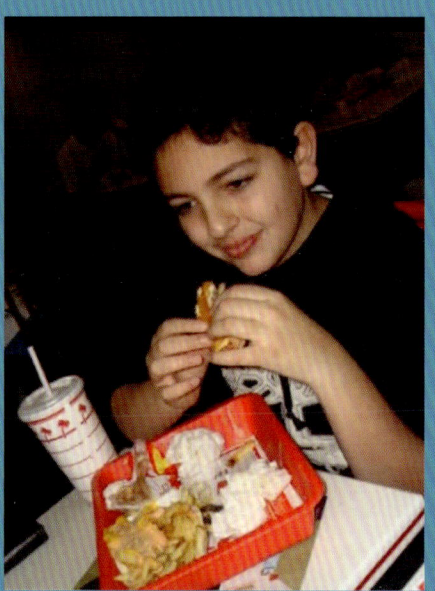

MY STORY

When I was growing up, my weight was a big insecurity.
I'd wear layers of compression shirts to hide my chest,
avoid talking to girls because I didn't feel confident,
and steer clear of pool parties to avoid anyone seeing
me without a shirt on. Food, especially fast food,
became my comfort. I'd indulge in McDonald's, Panda
Express, Jack in the Box, Chipotle, and Popeyes
because these places felt like momentary escapes
where I could feel good, even for just a little while.

At 18, I decided it was time for a change. I wanted
to feel better in my own skin, but I didn't want to give
up the foods I loved. That's when I discovered
macro-friendly cooking. It unlocked a new world:
Taking the foods I craved and making simple swaps to
reduce calories without sacrificing flavor. This
approach allowed me to enjoy every bite—from juicy
burgers to comforting pasta—while staying on track
with my goals. I lost 40 pounds by building these
healthier habits around eating, and the best part was
that I didn't feel deprived.

Cooking became more than just a skill; it became a
passion. I first got into cooking at 13, watching *Hell's
Kitchen* and learning from Gordon Ramsay's YouTube
videos. My first "win" in the kitchen was nailing a
steak, and from then on, I was hooked. When the
pandemic hit in 2020, I turned to TikTok to share my
love for cooking, showing others that they could also
enjoy great food and still reach their health goals.
I wanted people to see that eating healthy doesn't
mean giving up the foods you love.

I never expected my story to resonate with so
many, but it did. What began as a creative outlet
during a challenging time turned into a life-changing
journey. Four years later, an incredible community of
over six million followers across platforms continues
to inspire me to stick to my original mission: Helping
people eat good, live good, and make delicious food.

WHY DUPLICATE FAST FOOD?

Why create healthier versions of fast-food meals?
Here's the thing: About 36.6 percent of adults in the US—that's nearly 85 million people—eat fast food on any given day. It's popular for a reason. Fast food tastes great, and it's incredibly convenient. But let's be real, it's not the healthiest option. That's where this cookbook comes in. I wanted to create a way for people to enjoy those same familiar flavors but with a more health-conscious approach.

When I talk about "macro-friendly" cooking, I'm referring to the balance of macronutrients—proteins, carbs, and fats—that make up each meal. Protein is particularly important, especially for those who want to build muscle, stay fuller longer, or simply have more energy throughout the day. A high-protein diet can help with weight management, muscle repair, and overall satiety, which is why I've made sure every recipe in this cookbook is packed with protein to help you meet your goals without sacrificing flavor.

There's also a lot of nostalgia tied to fast food for me. When I was in high school, my main focuses were football and academics. I was extremely competitive and played defensive line, which meant long practices and grueling workouts. After practices, we were taught to refuel with plenty of food and protein, but my mom just couldn't keep up with the amount of food I needed to stay fueled. Fast food quickly became part of my weekly routine, with stops at places like Chipotle, Jack in the Box, McDonald's, and Panda Express. These meals became iconic for me: a comforting routine I'd look forward to after a hard practice.

This cookbook brings back those familiar flavors but in a healthier way. When I started my weight-loss journey, I realized I could still enjoy these foods by altering the recipes—using higher-protein ingredients paired with cooking methods that cut down on unnecessary calories and fats. Each chapter is organized to make it easy to find what you're craving, whether it's breakfast, lunch, dinner, or sweet treats. The recipes in this book aren't just recipes; they're reimagined versions of meals I grew up with, meals that have a special place in my story.

My goal is to make this cookbook a staple in every household, and help people reshape their approach to food while ensuring they still enjoy every bite. It's all about getting the best of both worlds: making meals that help you stay on track with your health goals and bringing back the flavors and comforts of those classic fast-food meals.

HOW TO USE THIS BOOK

This cookbook is designed for everyday use, with easy methods for incorporating high-protein, balanced meals into your routine. I've focused on creating macro-friendly recipes that don't take a lot of time, so they fit perfectly into a busy lifestyle. Whether you're an athlete looking to stay fueled or someone who wants simple, guilt-free weeknight meals, there's something here for you. My recommendation? Pick three to four recipes that you love and get really good at making them. Cycle them through your weekly meal plans, and when you're ready for something new, dive back into the book for more ideas. This approach not only saves time but also keeps your meals exciting and fresh. The recipes are structured to be easy to follow, with simple ingredients and clear steps to ensure you don't spend hours in the kitchen. You'll also find that these meals aren't just healthy but genuinely delicious, which makes sticking to your goals a lot more enjoyable. With these recipes, you can eat great food, meet your nutritional needs, and never feel like you're sacrificing flavor.

 If you'd like to know a recipe's full nutritional info and macros, scan this QR code with your smartphone. It will lead you to a list that contains all of this information for every recipe in this cookbook.

ESSENTIAL INGREDIENTS

To get the most out of these recipes, you'll want to keep these essential ingredients in your kitchen:

SEASONINGS

- ☐ Salt
- ☐ Pepper
- ☐ Garlic powder
- ☐ Onion powder
- ☐ Paprika
- ☐ Cayenne pepper
- ☐ Chili powder
- ☐ Taco seasoning

OILS

- ☐ **Olive oil:** Use extra-virgin for dressings, regular for low-heat cooking.
- ☐ **Avocado oil:** My go-to for high-heat cooking.
- ☐ **Beef tallow:** Adds a rich, savory flavor—great for frying or roasting.
- ☐ **Ghee:** Ideal for frying and imparting a rich, nutty flavor.
- ☐ **Butter:** Perfect for basting and adding a rich finish to meats or veggies.

PROTEINS

- ☐ **Chicken:** Boneless, skinless breasts or thighs.

  If using chicken breasts, remember they dry out quicker.
- ☐ **Beef:**

  Filet mignon: Tender and buttery.

  Top sirloin: Lean with bold flavor.

  Flat iron steak: Underrated, flavorful, and juicy.

HOW TO COOK THE PERFECT STEAK

1. **Pat the steak dry** to help it sear.
2. **Season** with salt, pepper, and garlic powder.
3. **Sear** in avocado oil on high heat in a heavy-bottom pan, 2 to 3 minutes per side.
4. **Lower the heat** to medium-low and add butter, garlic, rosemary, and thyme to baste for another 2 to 3 minutes.
5. **Remove the steak** from the pan and place on a wire rack or on an upside-down spoon on a plate. Let the steak rest for 6 to 8 minutes under a loose foil tent to keep the crust intact and allow the steak to finish cooking. For medium-rare, remove at 130°F and let rest to 135°F.

ESSENTIAL TOOLS

Here's a comprehensive list of essential tools to elevate your home cooking, making meal prep and everyday cooking more efficient and enjoyable:

Air Fryer: A game changer for quick, healthy meals with less oil. It's perfect for crisping up veggies, cooking proteins like chicken or fish, and making fries or snacks in a fraction of the time.

Nonstick skillet: Great for cooking eggs, pancakes, or delicate foods like fish. It's easy to clean and ideal for low-fat cooking since you need less oil.

Cast-iron skillet: Retains heat well and is perfect for searing meats before transferring to the oven. It's versatile for anything from steaks to baked dishes like cornbread.

Digital meat thermometer: Helps cook meat to the perfect temperature, ensuring it's safe to eat and not overcooked.

Cutting boards (wood and plastic): A wooden board for dry ingredients, and a plastic one for raw meats to prevent cross-contamination.

Chef's knife: A sharp, high-quality chef's knife for efficient chopping, slicing, and dicing.

Paring knife: Handy for peeling, trimming, and slicing small fruits and vegetables.

Measuring cups and spoons: Help ensure accurate measurements so recipes turn out just right, especially for baking.

Mixing bowls (various sizes): Make meal prep, mixing, and serving easier.

Tongs: Great for flipping meats, tossing salads, or grilling. They offer better control than a spatula for larger food items.

Whisk: Perfect for mixing dressings, eggs, or sauces to achieve a smooth consistency.

Baking sheets: Ideal for roasting veggies, baking chicken, or making sheet pan dinners.

Blender or food processor: A blender for smoothies and sauces, and a food processor for chopping, making dough, and blending soups.

Pressure cooker or slow cooker: Excellent for hands-off cooking—perfect for soups, stews, and tenderizing tough cuts of meat.

Kitchen shears: Great for trimming meat, cutting herbs, or snipping through packaging.

Peeler: Makes it easy to remove skins from fruits and vegetables quickly.

Silicone spatulas: Ideal for mixing, stirring, and scraping bowls clean. They can handle high heat, so they're great for cooking in pans.

Salad spinner: Washes and dries greens effectively, ensuring your salad is crisp and not soggy.

Microplane or zester: Handy for zesting citrus or grating garlic, ginger, or Parmesan cheese.

Colander: Useful for draining pasta, rinsing grains, or washing produce.

Rolling pin: Great for baking and flattening chicken breasts or dough.

Grill pan: Helps achieve grill marks on meats and veggies indoors; ideal when an outdoor grill isn't available.

SAMPLE MEAL PLANS

Here are a few meal plans using recipes from the cookbook. Each one is balanced with plenty of protein and flavor to help you stay on track.

MEAL PLAN 1
Breakfast: Healthy Oat-Flour Carrot Cake, (pg. 189)
Lunch: Barbecue Chicken Pizza with Lavash Bread, (pg. 118)
Snack: Firecracker Salmon Bites, (pg. 174)
Dinner: Big Mac Smash Tacos, (pg. 128)

MEAL PLAN 2
Breakfast: Cinnamon-Roll Protein Pancakes, (pg. 40)
Lunch: Honey-Chipotle Chicken Rice Bowl, (pg. 166)
Snack: Healthier Bang Bang Chicken Bites, (pg. 61)
Dinner: High-Protein Mac 'n' Cheese, (pg. 169)

MEAL PLAN 3
Breakfast: Copycat Sausage and Egg McMuffin, (pg. 31)
Lunch: Copycat Del Taco Chicken Soft Tacos, (pg. 123)
Snack: Oreo Milkshake, (pg. 199)
Dinner: One-Pan Lemon-Chicken Orzo Pasta, (pg. 163)

MEAL PLAN 4
Breakfast: Chocolate-Chip Baked Oats, (pg. 39)
Lunch: Lower-Calorie California Burrito, (pg. 105)
Snack: Garlic-Parmesan Wings, (pg. 66)
Dinner: Healthier One-Pot Lasagna Bowl, (pg. 173)

MEAL PLAN 5
Breakfast: Copycat Starbucks Spinach, Feta & Egg White Wrap, (pg. 35)
Lunch: Healthier Copycat In-N-Out Double-Double, (pg. 150)
Snack: High-Protein, Low-Calorie Loaded Nachos, (pg. 56)
Dinner: Healthier Fish & Chips, (pg. 177)

Meal Plan 1

EXQUISITE EATS INTRODUCTION

SAUCE CHEAT SHEET

These versatile sauces are easy to whip up and help elevate any meal, from tacos and salads to stir-fries and grilled meats. Each sauce brings unique flavors, whether you're craving spicy, creamy, or tangy. They're perfect for meal prep or last-minute dinners.

HONEY-GARLIC SOY SAUCE

Yield: Makes 1 cup
Prep time: 5 minutes
Cook time: 5 minutes
Total time: 10 minutes

~~~~~~~~~

Great for stir-fries, marinades, or drizzling over veggies. Try it with the Copycat Panda Express Teriyaki Chicken (pg. 162) or the Chinese Takeout Fried Rice (pg. 93).

~~~~~~~~~

½ cup low-sodium soy sauce
4 tbsp honey
4 garlic cloves, minced
2 tbsp rice vinegar
2 tsp sesame oil
¼ tsp salt
¼ tsp black pepper
1 tbsp cornstarch

1. **Mix.** In a small saucepan, whisk together the soy sauce, honey, garlic, rice vinegar, sesame oil, salt, and pepper.
2. **Heat.** In a small bowl, mix the cornstarch with ½ cup of cold water until smooth, then add the cornstarch slurry to the saucepan. Cook over medium heat until thickened, 4 to 5 minutes.

SPICY BANG BANG SAUCE

Yield: Makes 1¼ cups
Prep time: 5 minutes
Cook time: 0 minutes
Total time: 5 minutes

~~~~~~~~~

A versatile sauce for tacos, burgers, or roasted veggies. Try it on any of the salad recipes in this book, along with the Lower-Calorie California Burrito (pg. 105) or the Honey-Chipotle Chicken Rice Bowl (pg. 166).

~~~~~~~~~

1 cup plain nonfat Greek yogurt
2 tbsp sriracha (or hot sauce of choice)
2 tbsp lime juice
2 tsp honey
½ tsp smoked paprika
¼ tsp salt

1. To a blender or a small bowl, add all the ingredients and blend or whisk until smooth.

CREAMY CHIPOTLE SAUCE

Yield: Makes 1 cup
Prep time: 8 minutes
Cook time: 0 minutes
Total time: 8 minutes

~~~~~~~~~

Perfect for tacos, burritos, or as a dip. Try it with the Popcorn Shrimp (pg. 59) or the Chicken Tenders (pg. 62).

~~~~~~~~~

1 cup plain nonfat Greek yogurt
2–4 chipotle peppers in adobo sauce
2 tbsp lime juice
2 tsp garlic powder
¼ tsp salt

1. To a blender, add all the ingredients and blend until smooth, 45 seconds to 1 minute.

CILANTRO AVOCADO SAUCE

Yield: Makes 1½ cups
Prep time: 10 minutes
Cook time: 0 minutes
Total time: 10 minutes

~~~~~~~~~

Ideal for salads, wraps, and grilled chicken, or as a spread. Try it with the Mexican-Inspired Loaded Baked Potato (pg. 77) or the Healthier Baja Fish Tacos (pg. 132).

~~~~~~~~~

2 ripe avocados
1 cup plain nonfat Greek yogurt
1 cup fresh cilantro leaves
2 garlic cloves
Juice of 2 limes
¼ tsp salt

1. To a blender, add all the ingredients and blend until smooth, 45 seconds to 1 minute.

GARLICKY WHITE SAUCE

Yield: Makes 1½ cups
Prep time: 5 minutes
Cook time: 0 minutes
Total time: 5 minutes

~~~~~~~~~

Use as a dressing for salads or as a sauce for grilled meats. Try it on any of the salad recipes in this book, along with the Chicken Shawarma Wrap (pg. 103) or the Grilled Kofta Pita Pockets (pg. 108).

~~~~~~~~~

1 cup plain nonfat Greek yogurt
4 tbsp light mayo
4 garlic cloves, crushed
2 tbsp lemon juice
¼ tsp salt
¼ tsp black pepper
¼ tsp dried thyme
¼ tsp dried oregano
¼ tsp chili flakes (optional)

1. In a small bowl, mix together all the ingredients until well combined.

FREEZING AND STORING INSTRUCTIONS

To Store: Store any of these sauces in an airtight container in the fridge for up to 5 days. Stir or shake before serving as some ingredients may settle.

To Freeze: Freeze sauces like the Honey-Garlic Soy Sauce, Spicy Bang Bang Sauce, and Creamy Chipotle Sauce in airtight containers or ice cube trays for up to 3 months. Thaw in the fridge overnight and stir well before use. Avoid freezing the Cilantro Avocado Sauce as the avocados can discolor and affect the texture.

BREAKFAST
BREAKFAST
BREAKFAST
BREAKFAST
BREAKFAST
BREAKFAST
BREAKFAST

COPYCAT STARBUCKS KALE & MUSHROOM EGG BITES

The Kale & Mushroom Egg Bites are my second-favorite egg bites at Starbucks, but I order them more often because they're super nutritious and still taste insanely good. Plus, they're a great way to sneak in some greens first thing in the morning. These egg bites are light, fluffy, and full of umami flavor from the mushrooms and Parmesan. If you're looking for something delicious and packed with nutrients, these egg bites are a must-try. They're seriously so good!

Yield: Makes 12
Prep time: 15 minutes
Cook time: 25 minutes
Total time: 40 minutes

1 portabella mushroom, diced

1 tsp minced garlic

2 cups finely chopped kale

6 large eggs

1¼ cups low-fat cottage cheese

¼ cup low-fat mozzarella cheese

3 tbsp grated Parmesan cheese

½ tsp salt

¼ tsp black pepper

1. **Preheat the oven** to 350°F. Spray a 12-cup muffin tin or silicone molds with nonstick cooking spray.

2. **Sauté the vegetables.** Spray a medium skillet with nonstick cooking spray and place over medium heat. Sauté the mushroom and garlic for 5 to 8 minutes until tender. Add the kale and cook for another 3 to 5 minutes until wilted.

3. **Blend the egg mixture.** In a blender, combine the eggs, cottage cheese, mozzarella, Parmesan, salt, and pepper. Blend until smooth.

4. **Fill the molds.** Evenly distribute the veggie mixture into each mold, then pour the egg mixture over top, filling each to about three-quarters full.

5. **Bake.** Bake the egg bites for 20 to 25 minutes until they are set and the tops are slightly golden. They should have a slight jiggle in the center and be mostly set on the outside.

6. **Serve.** Allow the egg bites to cool for 10 minutes before removing from the molds. Serve warm.

Storage and Reheating Instructions: These egg bites can be stored in the fridge or frozen and reheated later. If reheating from frozen, wrap in a damp paper towel and microwave for 3 minutes, or until heated through.

COPYCAT STARBUCKS BACON & GRUYÈRE EGG BITES

When I first tried Starbucks's Bacon & Gruyère Egg Bites, I was hooked—the combination of the creamy, sharp cheese and smoky bacon were unreal. Growing up, I wasn't into eggs, but these changed the game. Plus, making them at home is way more wallet friendly. These egg bites have all the bomb flavors in a quick breakfast bite. If you're looking for a delicious and budget-friendly version of a Starbucks classic, you've got to try making these Gruyère bites yourself!

Yield: Makes 12
Prep time: 10 minutes
Cook time: 25 minutes
Total time: 35 minutes

4 slices bacon

6 large eggs

1¼ cups low-fat cottage cheese

1¼ cups shredded Gruyère (or a blend of Gruyère, cheddar, or Monterey Jack)

2 tbsp cornstarch

⅛ tsp black pepper

½ tsp hot sauce

¾ tsp salt

1. **Preheat the oven** to 375°F. Thoroughly spray a 12-cup muffin tin or silicone molds with nonstick cooking spray. (Silicone molds work well for a softer texture, but a muffin tin creates crispier edges.)

2. **Cook the bacon.** In a skillet over medium heat, cook the bacon for 5 to 7 minutes, until crispy. Crumble into small pieces and set aside.

3. **Blend the egg mixture.** In a blender, combine the eggs, cottage cheese, shredded cheese, cornstarch, black pepper, hot sauce, and salt. Blend until smooth.

4. **Fill the molds.** Pour the egg mixture evenly into the molds, filling each to about three-quarters full, then top with the crispy bacon bits.

5. **Bake.** Bake the egg bites for about 25 minutes until they are set and the tops are slightly golden. For crispier edges, broil the egg bites for 1 to 2 minutes after baking, watching closely to prevent burning.

6. **Serve.** Allow the egg bites to cool slightly before removing from the molds. Serve warm.

Storage and Reheating Instructions: These egg bites can be stored in the fridge or frozen and reheated later. Store in an airtight container in the fridge for up to 5 days and microwave on high for 30 to 60 seconds to reheat. Freeze individually wrapped in plastic wrap for up to 3 months. To reheat, microwave on low for 1 to 2 minutes, then high for 30 to 60 seconds, or reheat in an oven at 350°F for 10 to 15 minutes.

Note: If Gruyère is unavailable, substitute with Swiss cheese or another mild, nutty cheese like Emmental or Fontina.

Cheesy, fluffy bites of breakfast heaven!

HASH BROWNS

You won't believe how good these healthier hash browns are! They're just as crunchy and flavorful as McDonald's but are made in an air fryer, so they're way better for you while still packing that addictive bite. Plus, they're super easy to make, so you can enjoy a healthier version of your favorite fast-food hash browns anytime! These can be stored in the fridge or frozen and reheated later.

Yield: Makes 12
Prep time: 20 minutes
Cook time: 30 minutes
Chill time: 2 hours
Total time: 2 hours and 50 minutes

2 large potatoes
1 tbsp butter
1 tsp salt
¼ tsp garlic powder
1 tbsp potato starch
1 tbsp cornstarch
3 tbsp rice flour
1 tbsp water (plus more if needed)
Avocado oil (for frying)

1. **Prepare the potatoes.** Peel and grate the potatoes using a box grater. Transfer to a large bowl with ice water and let soak for 20 minutes. Drain the water and squeeze out as much moisture from the potatoes as possible using a clean kitchen towel or cheesecloth.
2. **Cook the shredded potatoes.** Heat a nonstick pan over medium heat and add the butter. Add the shredded potatoes and cook for 15 minutes, stirring occasionally, until tender.
3. **Make the hash brown dough.** Transfer the cooked potatoes to a bowl and let them cool slightly. Add the salt, garlic powder, potato starch, cornstarch, rice flour, and water. Mix until a thick dough forms. If the dough is too thick, add a splash of water.
4. **Shape the hash browns.** Using your hands, shape the mixture into rectangular hash browns approximately 3 inches long, 1½ inches wide, and ½ inch thick. Line a tray with parchment paper and place the hash browns on it. Refrigerate for at least 2 hours to firm up.
5. **Fry the hash browns.** In a large nonstick pan or pot over medium heat, heat about 1 inch of avocado oil. Once the oil is hot, carefully add the chilled hash browns and cook for 2 to 3 minutes on each side, or until golden and crispy.
6. **Serve.** Transfer the cooked hash browns to a wire rack to cool slightly before serving.

Storage and Reheating Instructions: Store cooked hash browns in an airtight container in the fridge for up to 4 days. Reheat in a skillet over medium heat with a drizzle of oil. Cook until heated through and crispy again. Freeze uncooked hash browns for up to 3 months. Flash freeze the shaped hash browns on a tray, then transfer them to an airtight container or freezer bag for longer storage.

4-INGREDIENT PROTEIN EVERYTHING BAGEL

Who doesn't love a bagel? The only issue is they're not the most calorie-friendly option—which is okay sometimes, but if you have a fitness plan, you gotta be disciplined. Enter these 4-Ingredient Protein Everything Bagels! They're easy to make, fluffy, and perfect for a quick protein-packed breakfast or snack. All you need is self-rising flour, Greek yogurt, and everything bagel seasoning. Mix, shape, bake, and you're done! Trust me, you'll be hooked!

Yield: Makes 4
Prep time: 10 minutes
Cook time: 25 minutes
Total time: 35 minutes

1 cup plain nonfat Greek yogurt
1 cup self-rising flour
1 egg, beaten (optional, for egg wash)
Everything bagel seasoning

1. **Preheat the oven** to 375°F and line a baking sheet with parchment paper.
2. **Make the dough.** In a medium mixing bowl, combine the Greek yogurt and flour. Stir until a dough forms. Turn the dough out onto a lightly floured surface and knead until smooth. Use a little extra flour, if necessary, to prevent sticking.
3. **Divide and shape the dough.** Divide the dough into 4 equal parts.
   Option 1: Roll each piece into a rope, then connect the ends to form a bagel shape.
   Option 2: Roll each piece into a ball, poke a hole in the center, and stretch it out to form the bagel.
   Each bagel should be approximately 3 to 4 inches in diameter after shaping.
4. **Apply the egg wash (if using).** Brush the top of each bagel with the egg wash. This will help the seasoning stick and give the bagels a golden color when baked.
5. **Add the seasoning.** Generously sprinkle the everything bagel seasoning over the bagels.
6. **Bake.** Place the bagels onto the lined baking sheet. Bake for 20 to 25 minutes, or until golden brown.
7. **Cool and serve.** Allow the bagels to cool on a wire rack, then serve.

Storage and Reheating Instructions: To keep bagels fresh, store them in an airtight container at room temperature for up to 2 days or refrigerate for up to 4 days. Reheat in a toaster oven for best results.

Drip check!

COPYCAT SAUSAGE & EGG MCMUFFIN

When I was growing up, my mom would take my sister and me to McDonald's early in the morning on our way to school, and I fell in love with the iconic McDonald's Sausage and Egg McMuffin. This version is high in protein and low in calories, and tastes just as good as the original. Because its components can be prepped and stored in advance, it's super convenient for those busy mornings when you need a quick meal. You can make a batch ahead of time, and enjoy a delicious, healthy breakfast all week long.

Yield: Makes 5
Prep time: 15 minutes
Cook time: 20 minutes
Total time: 35 minutes

FOR SAUSAGE PATTIES

8oz (93% lean) ground beef
8oz (93% lean) ground pork
¾ tsp salt
½ tsp black pepper
½ tsp garlic powder
½ tsp onion powder
¼ tsp dried basil
¼ tsp dried oregano
¼ tsp dried thyme
½ tsp fennel seeds
1 tsp cornstarch or
   arrowroot starch

FOR ASSEMBLY

1 tbsp butter
5 eggs
Salt and pepper, to taste
5 English muffins
5 Velveeta slices (or your
   preferred cheese)

1. **Prepare the sausage patties.** In a large bowl, mix together the ground beef, ground pork, salt, black pepper, garlic powder, onion powder, dried basil, dried oregano, dried thyme, fennel seeds and cornstarch. Form the mixture into 5 equal-size patties, approximately 3½ inches in diameter and ½ inch thick to fit the English muffins properly.

2. **Cook the sausage patties.** Heat a large nonstick skillet over medium heat, spray with avocado oil, and add the patties. Cook for 4 to 5 minutes per side, until browned and cooked through. Remove the patties from the skillet and set aside. Wipe out the pan with a paper towel to avoid transferring excess grease to the eggs.

3. **Cook the eggs.** In the same skillet, melt the butter and fry each egg separately to your desired doneness. (I like mine over easy or sunny-side up!) Season with salt and pepper.

4. **Assemble the McMuffins.** Toast the English muffins. Place a sausage patty, a cooked egg, and a slice of Velveeta, in that order, on each muffin.

5. **Serve.** Enjoy the McMuffin right away or wrap it up for a quick, on-the-go breakfast.

Storage and Reheating Instructions: To freeze, assemble the muffins (including cheese) and wrap individually in foil or plastic wrap. Freeze in an airtight container or freezer bag for up to 3 months. To reheat, remove wrapping, wrap in a damp paper towel, and microwave on medium for 1 to 2 minutes, (2 to 3 minutes if frozen), or until heated through. For crispiness, reheat in a toaster oven at 350°F for 8 to 10 minutes (from frozen).

COPYCAT MCGRIDDLE

The delightful mix of sweet and savory in a McGriddle is hard to beat, but this version takes it up a notch with higher protein content. You'll still get all the mouthwatering flavors you crave but in a healthier and more budget-friendly package. By making these at home, you can enjoy a nutritious breakfast that aligns with your fitness goals, while also being able to prepare a batch in advance for convenience throughout the week. It's incredibly satisfying, even with the lighter ingredients.

Yield: Makes 5
Prep time: 25 minutes
Cook time: 30 minutes
Total time: 55 minutes

FOR THE PANCAKE BUNS
1 cup oat flour, or all-purpose flour
1 tsp baking powder
½ tsp salt
2 eggs
½ cup 2% milk
¼ cup plain nonfat Greek yogurt
10 tbsp sugar-free syrup

FOR THE FILLING
1lb lean ground sausage
5 eggs
Salt and pepper, to taste
5 Velveeta slices, or low-fat
   cheese slices of your preference
5 tbsp sugar-free syrup

1. **Make the pancake batter.** In a medium bowl, mix together the flour, baking powder, and salt. In a separate medium bowl, mix the eggs, milk, and Greek yogurt until smooth. Combine the wet ingredients with the dry, and mix until you have a thick pancake batter—don't overmix; a few lumps are okay! Let the batter rest for 10 minutes before cooking. (This allows the flour to absorb fully, resulting in fluffier pancakes.)

2. **Cook the pancake buns.** Heat a medium nonstick skillet over medium heat for 3 to 5 minutes, then spray lightly with avocado oil. Pour ¼ cup of the pancake batter into the skillet to form a small pancake, then immediately top with 1 tablespoon sugar-free syrup. Cook until bubbles just begin to form on the surface of the pancake buns, then flip and cook for another minute. Repeat to make 10 pancakes.

3. **Prepare the filling.** Shape the ground sausage into 5 patties. Heat a large skillet over medium-high heat, and add the patties. Cook for 4 to 5 minutes per side, until browned and cooked through, then set aside to cool. In the same skillet, fry each egg separately to your desired doneness (I like mine sunny-side up!), 4 to 5 minutes over medium-high heat. For sunny-side up, don't flip the egg; simply let cook until the whites on top are just set. About a minute before the eggs are done cooking, place a Velveeta slice on each egg to melt. Allow the eggs to cook fully as the cheese melts.

4. **Assemble the McGriddles.** Top 1 pancake with a sausage patty, a fried egg with melted cheese, and a tablespoon of syrup. Place another pancake on top to complete the sandwich. Repeat with the remaining ingredients.

5. **Serve.** Enjoy the McGriddle right away or wrap it up for a quick breakfast on the go.

Storage and Reheating Instructions: To freeze, assemble the McGriddles (including cheese), and wrap individually in foil or plastic wrap. Freeze in an airtight container or freezer bag for up to 3 months. To reheat, remove wrapping, wrap in a damp paper towel, and microwave on medium for 1 to 2 minutes (2 to 3 minutes if frozen), or until heated through. For crispiness, reheat in a toaster oven at 350°F for 8 to 10 minutes (from frozen).

COPYCAT STARBUCKS SPINACH, FETA & EGG WHITE WRAP

When I first tried the Starbucks Spinach, Feta & Egg White Wrap, I couldn't believe how good it was. But spending money at Starbucks every day really adds up, which is why I made this version at home. It's just as delicious, healthier, and much more budget friendly. Packed with protein, thanks to the egg whites and feta, and filled with nutritious spinach, this wrap is perfect for a satisfying breakfast or snack. Now I can enjoy my favorite wrap anytime without breaking the bank!

Yield: Makes 1
Prep time: 5 minutes
Cook time: 7 minutes
Total time: 12 minutes

¼ cup chopped fresh spinach
3 large egg whites
¼ tsp salt
¼ tsp black pepper
¼ cup crumbled feta cheese
1 (8in) whole-wheat tortilla or
   1 piece of Lavash bread

1. **Cook the spinach.** Heat a medium nonstick skillet over medium heat, and spray with olive oil. Add the spinach and cook for 1 to 2 minutes, until wilted.
2. **Add the egg whites.** In the skillet, pour the egg whites over the spinach. Season with salt and pepper, and cook, stirring occasionally for 3 to 5 minutes, until the egg whites are fully set.
3. **Warm the tortilla.** While the egg whites are cooking, in a separate large skillet, warm the tortilla. Alternatively, microwave for 10 to 20 seconds with a damp paper towel.
4. **Assemble the wrap.** Sprinkle the crumbled feta cheese over the cooked egg whites. Place the egg, spinach, and feta mixture onto the center of the warmed tortilla. Fold the bottom of the tortilla up over the filling, then fold in the sides and roll tightly.
5. **Serve.** Cut the wrap in half, if desired, and serve warm.

Storage and Reheating Instructions: To freeze, assemble the wrap, wrap tightly in foil, and freeze in an airtight container or freezer bag for up to 3 months. To reheat in the oven, remove foil and bake at 350°F for 15 to 20 minutes, or until heated through. To reheat in a microwave, remove foil, wrap in a damp paper towel, and microwave on medium power for 2 to 3 minutes from frozen, or until warmed through. To reheat in an air fryer, preheat the air fryer to 350°F. Place the frozen wrap in the air-fryer basket and heat for 10 to 12 minutes, flipping halfway through, until warmed through and crispy on the outside.

COPYCAT PHILZ GREEN CHILE BURRITO

Philz is legit my favorite coffee in the world, but when I tried their Green Chile Burrito, I was *blown away*! The flavors are absolutely incredible and have the perfect combination of creamy, tangy, and cheesy. Plus, it's super easy to make and perfect for meal prepping. You can whip up a batch and enjoy these amazing burritos all week long. If you love a good burrito, you're going to be obsessed with this one!

Yield: Makes 6
Prep time: 10 minutes
Cook time: 10 minutes
Total time: 20 minutes

1 tbsp butter

12 large eggs, beaten

½ cup salsa verde

1 container hatch chiles

6oz frozen tater tots, cooked according to package instructions

5 slices cooked crispy bacon, crumbled

2 cups low-fat shredded cheddar cheese

6 low-carb flour tortillas

1. **Cook the eggs.** In a large skillet over medium-high heat, add the butter and allow it to melt. Add in the beaten eggs, and scramble gently for 3 to 5 minutes, or until your desired doneness. (I prefer a softer scramble, around 4 minutes of cooking.) Two minutes before the eggs are cooked to your desired doneness, mix in the salsa verde and hatch chiles. Mixing the salsa directly into the scrambled eggs will enhance the flavor and moisture.

2. **Combine the ingredients.** To the skillet with the scrambled eggs, add the cooked tater tots and crumbled bacon, stirring to combine. Sprinkle the shredded cheddar over the egg mixture and allow it to melt for 3 to 5 minutes.

3. **Assemble the burritos.** Warm the flour tortillas in the microwave for 30 seconds with a damp towel to make them pliable. Divide the egg-and-tater-tot mixture evenly among the tortillas. Fold the bottom of each tortilla up over the filling, then fold in the sides and roll tightly.

4. **Serve.** Serve the burritos hot, with additional salsa on the side if desired.

Storage and Reheating Instructions: To freeze, assemble the burritos, wrap tightly in foil or plastic wrap, and freeze in an airtight container or freezer bag for up to 3 months. To reheat in a microwave, remove wrapping, wrap in a damp paper towel, and microwave for 2 to 3 minutes from frozen. To reheat in an air fryer, preheat to 350°F, place the burritos in the air fryer basket, and heat for 8 to 10 minutes, flipping halfway through.

Note: If hatch green chiles are unavailable, add ¼ cup more salsa verde.

A soft, gooey-chocolate surprise in every bite!

CHOCOLATE-CHIP BAKED OATS

This chocolate-chip baked oats recipe went viral on TikTok, and when I tried it, I was blown away. I never knew something as boring as oats could taste so good and indulgent! It's like having cake for breakfast but without the guilt. Seriously, it's mind-blowing how delicious and easy it is. Just mix everything up, bake it, and *boom*—dessert for breakfast! If you haven't tried this recipe yet, you're missing out big time.

Yield: Serves 1
Prep time: 5 minutes
Cook time: 25 minutes
Total time: 30 minutes

½ ripe medium banana (or ¼ cup applesauce or pumpkin purée), mashed

½ cup oats (quick, minute, or rolled all work)

1 medium egg

½ tsp baking powder

1 tsp vanilla extract

½ tbsp maple syrup

1 tbsp peanut butter

Small handful of semi-sweet chocolate chips of your preferred type (milk or dark)

½ tsp cinnamon (optional)

1. **Preheat the oven** to 350°F.
2. **Combine the ingredients.** In a medium mixing bowl, combine the mashed banana, oats, egg, baking powder, vanilla extract, maple syrup, and peanut butter. Stir until well combined. Mix in the chocolate chips and cinnamon (if using).
3. **Prepare the baking dish.** Lightly grease a small, round oven-safe dish (approximately 5 to 6 inches in diameter) or line with parchment paper. Pour the oats mixture into the prepared baking dish.
4. **Bake.** Bake for 25 minutes, or until the top is golden and the oats are set.
5. **Serve.** Allow the baked oats to cool slightly before eating. Enjoy warm!

MACRO-FRIENDLY CINNAMON-ROLL PANCAKES

Growing up, cinnamon rolls were my favorite dessert, so I had to find a healthier way to enjoy them. These cinnamon-roll pancakes taste like a treat but keep you on track with your fitness goals. I use a mix of low-fat buttermilk, flour, and protein powder to keep them fluffy and satisfying. The cinnamon swirl and touch of sweetener make these pancakes feel indulgent, like you're having dessert for breakfast. Plus, the trick is steaming them with a lid instead of flipping to keep that swirl intact.

Yield: Makes 4
Prep time: 10 minutes
Cook time: 15 minutes
Total time: 25 minutes

FOR THE PANCAKES
¾ cup low-fat buttermilk
1 large egg
2 tbsp light butter, melted
1½ tsp vanilla extract
¾ cup all-purpose flour
¼ cup casein protein powder
   (vanilla or unflavored)
2 tbsp zero-calorie sweetener
1 tsp baking powder
½ tsp baking soda
½ tsp salt

FOR THE CINNAMON-SWIRL FILLING
5½ tbsp packed brown sugar
¼ cup light butter, melted
1½ tsp ground cinnamon

FOR THE CREAM-CHEESE ICING
2 tbsp light butter, softened
2oz light cream cheese
½ cup powdered sugar substitute
   (Swerve Confectioners')
½ tsp vanilla extract

1. **Prepare the pancakes.** In a medium bowl, whisk together the low-fat buttermilk, egg, melted light butter, and vanilla extract. In another medium bowl, mix together the flour, casein protein powder, sweetener, baking powder, baking soda, and salt. Gradually combine the wet and dry ingredients until just moistened.

2. **Prepare the cinnamon-swirl filling.** In a small bowl, mix together the brown sugar, melted light butter, and cinnamon. Pour into a resealable bag or piping bag and refrigerate for about 10 minutes until thickened.

3. **Cook the pancakes.** Heat a nonstick griddle or skillet over medium heat and spray with cooking spray. Pour ⅓ cup of batter onto the griddle. Cook until bubbles appear, about 2 to 3 minutes.

4. **Add the cinnamon swirl.** Cut a small corner off the bag with the cinnamon filling and swirl it over the pancake, leaving some space around the edges. Cover the pancake with a lid and steam for 1 to 2 minutes. This helps set the swirl. Flip the pancake carefully and cook for another 30 to 45 seconds to lightly brown the other side. Repeat until all batter is used.

5. **Prepare the cream-cheese icing.** In a small, microwave-safe bowl, combine the light butter and cream cheese. Microwave in 10-second increments, stirring until smooth. Mix in the powdered sugar substitute and vanilla extract until creamy.

6. **Serve.** Drizzle the icing over the pancakes, and enjoy warm.

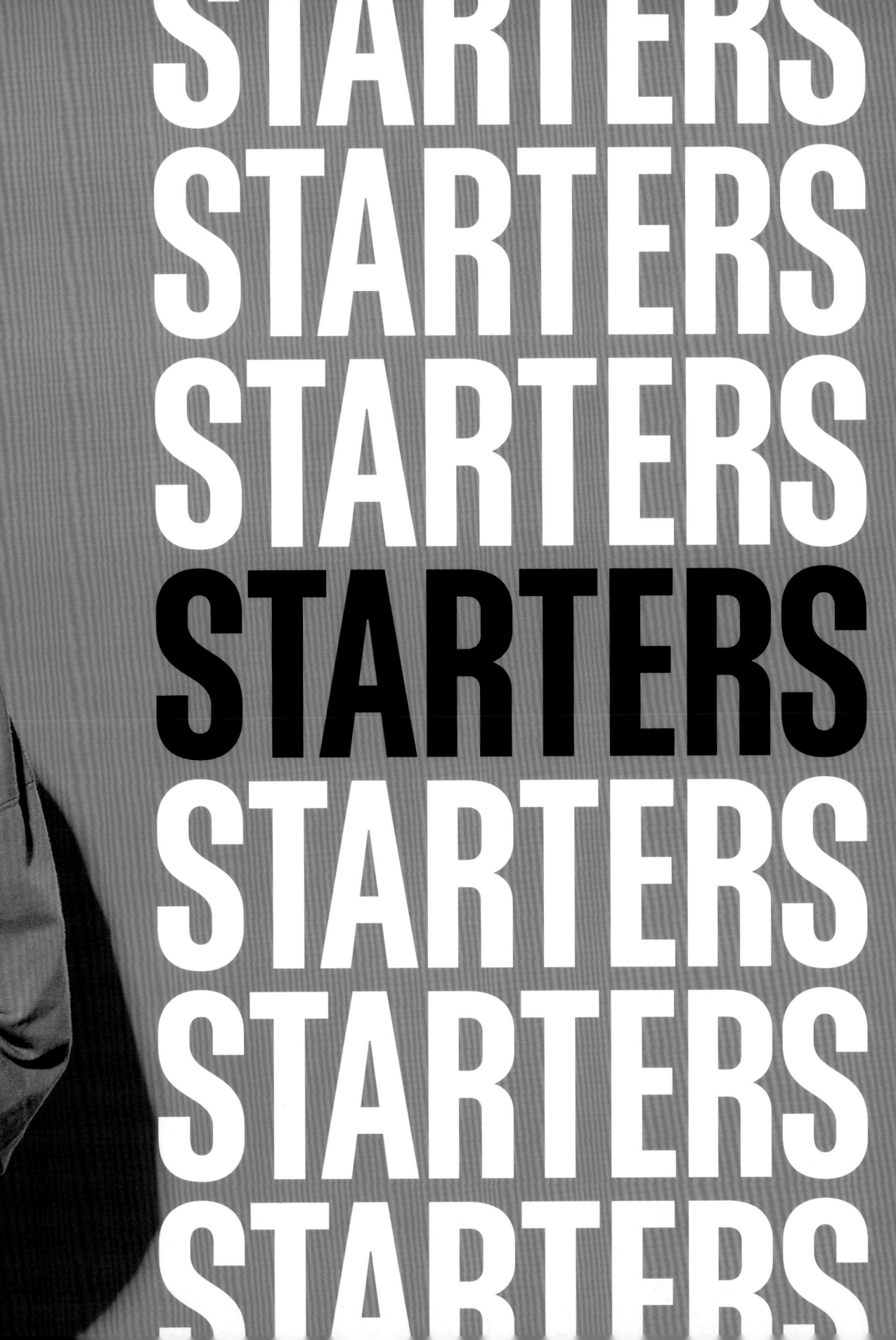

HIGH-PROTEIN, LOW-CALORIE GARLIC CHEESE BREAD

I never thought I'd say this, but High-Protein, Low-Calorie Garlic Cheese Bread is a thing! This version comes so close to the delicious flavors of real garlic bread that you'll be amazed. It's perfect for enjoying your favorite comfort food with less guilt. The cheesy, garlicky goodness is still there, and you won't feel like you're missing out at all. Who knew you could have your garlic bread and eat it too?

Yield: Makes 4
Prep time: 10 minutes
Cook time: 15 minutes
Total time: 25 minutes

¼ cup plain nonfat Greek yogurt
2 tbsp melted light butter
2–3 cloves garlic, minced
¼ cup grated Parmesan cheese
1 tsp dried parsley
½ tsp dried oregano
Salt and pepper, to taste
4 slices whole-grain bread, sourdough bread, or baguette
½ cup shredded low-fat mozzarella cheese
Chopped fresh parsley, to garnish (optional)

1. **Preheat the oven** to 375°F, and line a baking sheet with parchment paper.
2. **Prepare the garlic spread.** In a small bowl, combine the Greek yogurt, melted butter, minced garlic, grated Parmesan cheese, dried parsley, and dried oregano. Add salt and pepper to taste. Mix well to create a smooth garlic spread.
3. **Assemble the bread.** Spread the garlic mixture evenly over the slices of bread, using only as much spread as is needed to coat each piece.
4. **Add the cheese.** Top each slice of bread with an even layer of shredded mozzarella.
5. **Bake.** On a baking sheet lined with parchment paper, place the prepared bread slices. Bake for 10 to 15 minutes, or until the cheese is melted and bubbly and the edges of the bread are golden brown.
6. **Garnish and serve.** Remove the garlic bread from the oven and let cool slightly. Garnish with fresh chopped parsley (if using) for added color and freshness. Serve immediately.

LOADED BACON CHEDDAR FRIES

Nothing sounds healthy about loaded bacon cheddar fries, right? *Wrong.* My version uses substitutions that make this recipe nutritionally sound. We use air-fried fries, turkey bacon or center-cut bacon, and low-fat cheddar cheese, all drizzled with some low-cal ranch. You can't even tell it's "healthier." It's got all the indulgent flavors you love but without the extra calories. So, go ahead and enjoy these delicious fries!

Yield: Serves 2
Prep time: 15 minutes
Cook time: 5–7 minutes (Air Fryer) or 10–12 minutes (Oven)
Total time: 20–27 minutes

10oz lean ground beef or ground chicken

1 tsp taco seasoning

2 cups **Homemade Fast-Food Fries** (pg. 74)

¾ cup shredded low-fat or fat-free cheddar cheese

2–3 slices cooked crispy center-cut bacon (or turkey bacon), crumbled

2–3 tbsp yogurt ranch dressing

Green onions, sliced, for garnish (optional)

1. **Cook the ground meat.** Spray a large skillet with avocado oil, and place over medium heat. Add the ground beef and cook until browned and cooked through. With a few minutes of cook time remaining, sprinkle the taco seasoning over the ground beef and stir well to combine. Set aside.

2. **Preheat the oven** to 375°F, or the air fryer to 350°F.

3. **Assemble the fries.** To the bottom of an oven-safe dish or an air-fryer basket, layer the cooked fries. Evenly distribute the cooked meat over the fries, then sprinkle the cheddar cheese over top. Lastly, add the crumbled bacon.

4. **Heat the loaded fries.**
   Oven: Place the loaded fries into the oven and bake for 10 to 12 minutes, or until the cheese is melted and bubbly.
   Air fryer: Cook for 5 to 7 minutes or until the cheese has melted.

5. **Add the final toppings.** Once the cheese is melted and the fries are hot, remove from the oven or air fryer. Drizzle with yogurt ranch dressing and sprinkle sliced green onions on top for garnish (if using).

6. **Serve.** Enjoy the fries as a hearty snack or as part of a meal.

The ultimate cheesy, crispy indulgence!

LOW-CALORIE POUTINE

Okay, let me tell you why I love this Low-Calorie Poutine. It's super indulgent, has way fewer calories, and is ridiculously easy to make. Plus, you don't have to trek all the way to Canada to get your poutine fix. (No offense, Canada, but those flights aren't cheap!) With air-fried fries, melty low-fat cheese, and savory gravy, it's comfort food without the guilt. You'll be amazed at how delicious this dish is while still being healthy. Enjoy the best of both worlds, eh?

Yield: Serves 4
Prep time: 10 minutes
Cook time: 15–20 minutes (Air Fryer) or 25–30 minutes (Oven)
Total time: 25–40 minutes

FOR THE FRIES
4 large Russet potatoes, cut into ½-in thick sticks
2 tbsp olive oil
Salt and pepper, to taste

FOR THE POUTINE
1 cup shredded low-fat mozzarella cheese or cheese curds
2 cups low-sodium beef gravy (homemade or store-bought)

1. **Preheat the air fryer** to 400°F, or the oven to 425°F.
2. **Prepare and cook the fries.** In a large bowl, toss the potato sticks with olive oil, salt, and pepper.
    Air fryer: To the air-fryer basket, add the seasoned potatoes. Air-fry for 15 to 20 minutes, shaking the basket halfway through, until the fries are golden and crispy.
    Oven: To a large baking sheet, spread the seasoned potatoes in a single layer. Bake for 25 to 30 minutes, flipping halfway through, until the fries are golden and crispy.
3. **Heat the gravy.** While the fries are cooking, heat the beef gravy in a saucepan over medium heat until hot.
4. **Assemble the poutine.** Place the hot fries on a serving plate, evenly sprinkle mozzarella cheese over top, and pour hot gravy over the cheese and fries.
5. **Serve immediately.** Enjoy while it's hot and the cheese is melty.

Low-Calorie Poutine

Air-Fryer Mozzarella Sticks

AIR-FRYER MOZZARELLA STICKS

I can't get enough of mozzarella sticks, especially on game days or during UFC fights. This version is absolutely amazing! They've got all the cheesy, crunchy goodness you crave while still being a smart and healthy choice thanks to the low-fat mozzarella and the use of an air fryer rather than a deep fryer. These mozzarella sticks are packed with protein and are low in calories. Plus, they're super easy to make, and you'll get that epic cheese pull every single time. These are perfect for when you want to indulge and feel great about it afterward!

Yield: Makes 24
Prep time: 50 minutes
Cook time: 8 minutes
Total time: 58 minutes

12 low-fat mozzarella string cheese sticks, halved lengthwise
½ cup all-purpose flour
2 eggs
½ cup Italian breadcrumbs
½ cup panko breadcrumbs
½ cup grated Parmesan cheese
1 tsp garlic powder
1 tsp Italian seasoning
Cooking spray

1. **Set up the dredging station.** Arrange 3 shallow bowls for the dredging process. In the first bowl, place the all-purpose flour. In the second bowl, add the eggs and beat until well mixed. In the third bowl, mix together the breadcrumbs, grated Parmesan cheese, garlic powder, and Italian seasoning.

2. **Dredge the mozzarella sticks.** Coat each mozzarella stick in the flour first, shaking off any excess. Next, dip into the beaten eggs, ensuring complete coverage. Finally, roll in the breadcrumb mixture, pressing the crumbs to the stick to ensure they adhere well.

3. **Freeze the mozzarella sticks.** To a baking sheet lined with parchment paper, place the breaded mozzarella sticks and put in the freezer for at least 30 minutes to ensure the cheese is firm and the coating is set. This helps prevent them from melting too quickly when cooked.

4. **Preheat the air fryer** to 400°F while the mozzarella sticks freeze.

5. **Cook the mozzarella sticks.** Spray the air-fryer basket with nonstick cooking spray to prevent sticking. In the air-fryer basket, place the frozen mozzarella sticks in a single layer—you may need to work in batches depending on the size of your air fryer. Lightly spray the tops of the mozzarella sticks with cooking spray. Air-fry for 6 to 8 minutes, or until golden and crispy. (No need to flip during cooking.)

6. **Serve.** Serve hot with marinara or your favorite dipping sauce.

Note: These mozzarella sticks can be frozen and stored (before air-frying) for future cooking.

Golden, gooey, and totally irresistible!

LOW-CALORIE TORTILLA CHIPS

Who doesn't love a tasty tortilla chip? This version lets you enjoy them even more while staying on track with your health goals. These Low-Calorie Tortilla Chips are air-fried or baked to crispy perfection, making them a healthier choice compared to store-bought options. They're just as delicious and ideal for dipping in your favorite salsa or guacamole. Now you can snack on tortilla chips and feel good about every crunch!

Yield: Serves 2–3
Prep time: 5 minutes
Cook time: 5–7 minutes (Air Fryer) or 10–12 minutes (Oven)
Total time: 10–17 minutes

6–8 (8in) low-carb or
    corn tortillas
Cooking spray
Salt, to taste
Optional seasonings: garlic
    powder, chili powder, paprika

1. **Preheat the air fryer** to 350°F, or the oven to 375°F.
2. **Prepare the tortillas.** Stack the tortillas, and cut them into eighths to make chip-sized triangles. In an air-fryer basket or on a baking sheet, spread out the tortilla triangles in a single layer. Avoid overlapping the triangles to ensure even cooking. Lightly spray the tortillas with cooking spray. Sprinkle with salt and any seasonings you like, such as garlic powder, chili powder, or paprika.
3. **Cook the tortilla chips.**
   Air fryer: Cook for 5 to 7 minutes or until crisp, flipping the tortilla pieces halfway through to ensure even browning and prevent burning. You may need to work in batches depending on the size of your air fryer.
   Oven: Bake for 10 to 12 minutes, flipping the chips halfway through, until they are crisp and lightly golden.
4. **Cool and serve.** Remove the chips from the air fryer or oven, and let cool for a few minutes—they will continue to crisp up as they cool. Serve the chips alone or with your favorite low-calorie dip or salsa.

HIGH-PROTEIN, LOW-CALORIE LOADED NACHOS

I absolutely love munching on nachos while watching football games or UFC fights. It's easy to get carried away with the usual unhealthy versions, but this one lets you enjoy every bite and still feel great about it. Made with low-carb tortillas, these nachos are high in protein and low in calories. They're loaded with seasoned ground beef, melted cheese, and fresh toppings, giving you all the deliciousness and crunch without the extra calories. Perfect for game day—you can indulge and feel fantastic afterward!

Yield: Serves 3–4

Prep time: 15 minutes

Cook time: 5–7 minutes (Air Fryer) or 8–10 minutes (Oven)

Total Time: 20–25 minutes

1lb lean ground beef or ground chicken

2 tsp taco seasoning

½ cup black beans, drained and rinsed

½ cup corn (canned or fresh)

½ cup diced tomatoes

¼ cup diced red onion

¼ cup sliced black olives

¼ cup sliced jalapeños (fresh or pickled)

Low-Calorie Tortilla Chips (pg. 55)

1 cup shredded low-fat cheddar cheese

1 avocado, diced (optional)

Fresh cilantro, chopped, to garnish

Juice of 1 lime, to garnish

1 cup plain nonfat Greek yogurt, to serve

Salsa of preference, to serve

1. **Cook the meat.** To a large skillet over medium heat, add the ground beef and cook until browned and cooked through. Drain any excess fat. Stir in the taco seasoning and mix well. Set aside to cool slightly.

2. **Prepare the toppings.** In separate individual bowls, arrange the black beans, corn, diced tomatoes, diced red onion, sliced black olives, and sliced jalapeños.

3. **Preheat the air fryer** to 350°F, or the oven to 375°F.

4. **Layer the nachos.** On a baking sheet or in an air-fryer basket, spread out a layer of the Low-Calorie Tortilla Chips. Evenly distribute the cooked beef over the chips. Sprinkle the shredded cheese over top, then add layers of black beans, corn, tomatoes, red onions, black olives, and jalapeños.

5. **Cook the nachos.**
   Air fryer: Air-fry for 5 to 7 minutes, or until the cheese is melted and bubbly. This method works best for smaller, single-portion nachos.
   Oven: Bake for 8 to 10 minutes, or until the cheese is melted and bubbly. This method is best for larger batches.

6. **Add the final toppings.** Once cooked, remove the nachos from the air fryer or oven. Top with diced avocado (if using), a generous sprinkle of chopped cilantro, and a drizzle of lime juice.

7. **Serve.** Serve immediately with bowls of Greek yogurt and salsa on the side for dipping.

POPCORN SHRIMP

I absolutely adore these high-protein Popcorn Shrimp because they're not only indulgent and crispy but they're also full of protein. What's better? The popcorn shrimp taste so mouthwatering, you'd never know they're healthy. They're the perfect choice for a crunchy, satisfying snack or appetizer that's actually great for you. Plus, they're incredibly simple to make and utterly irresistible. You'll find yourself reaching for more, just like with popcorn!

Yield: Serves 4
Prep time: 10 minutes
Cook time: 10 minutes
Total time: 20 minutes

1lb (30–40) large raw shrimp,
   peeled and deveined, tails
   removed
½ cup all-purpose flour
½ tsp salt
½ tsp black pepper
2 eggs
2 cups panko breadcrumbs
1 tsp garlic powder
1 tsp paprika
Avocado oil spray

1. **Set up the dredging station.** Gather 3 shallow bowls. In the first bowl, combine the all-purpose flour, salt, and black pepper. In the second bowl, add the eggs and beat until well mixed. In the third bowl, mix together the panko breadcrumbs, garlic powder, and paprika.

2. **Dredge the shrimp.** Dip each shrimp into the flour mixture first. Make sure they are fully coated, then tap off the excess flour. Next, dip the flour-coated shrimp into the beaten eggs. Finally, coat the shrimp thoroughly with the seasoned panko mixture. Press lightly to ensure the breadcrumbs adhere well.

3. **Preheat the air fryer** to 400°F. Line a plate with paper towels.

4. **Cook the shrimp.** Lightly spray the breaded shrimp with cooking oil. To the air-fryer basket, add the shrimp in a single layer. Cook for 8 to 10 minutes until golden and crispy. Gently flip the shrimp halfway through and spray with cooking spray again to make them even crispier.

5. **Serve.** Serve hot with your choice of dips, such as cocktail sauce, tartar sauce, spicy mayo, or Creamy Chipotle Sauce (pg. 19).

Note: When preparing the raw shrimp, it's helpful to pat them dry with paper towels to remove any excess moisture.

CHICKEN NUGGETS

Growing up, I was a picky eater, which comes as a shock to most people. Chicken nuggets were one of the only foods I truly indulged in almost every night. This version would make my younger self proud. They're high in protein, lower in calories, and don't even taste "healthy." You get all the crispy, delicious goodness you remember but with a nutritional upgrade. Perfect for indulging your inner child while sticking to your health goals!

Yield: Makes 20
Prep time: 20 minutes
Cook time: 10–12 minutes (Air Fryer) or 18–20 minutes (Oven)
Total time: 30–40 minutes

1lb lean ground chicken
1 egg
½ cup shredded low-fat mozzarella
¾ tsp salt
½ tsp black pepper
1 tsp garlic powder
1 tsp onion powder
¼ tsp cayenne pepper (optional)
1½ cups cornflake breadcrumbs
Cooking spray

1. **Preheat the oven** to 400°F and line a baking sheet with parchment paper. If air-frying, preheat the air fryer to 375°F.
2. **Prepare the chicken mixture.** In a large bowl, mix together the ground chicken, egg, shredded mozzarella, salt, pepper, garlic powder, onion powder, and cayenne pepper (if using) until combined. The mixture will be wet and tacky; this is normal for achieving tender, juicy nuggets
3. **Form nuggets.** Shape the chicken into portions of about 2 to 3 tablespoons, and place on a plate.
4. **Dredge the nuggets.** To a small bowl, add the cornflake breadcrumbs. Coat each nugget in the breadcrumbs, and place on the lined baking sheet. If air-frying, place the nuggets in the air-fryer basket in a single layer.
5. **Cook the nuggets.**
   Air fryer: Cook in batches for 10 to 12 minutes, flipping halfway through and lightly spraying with cooking spray, until golden and cooked through to 165°F.
   Oven: Bake for 18 to 20 minutes on a wire rack set over a baking sheet, until golden and cooked through to 165°F. Flip halfway through and lightly spray the nuggets with cooking spray.
6. **Serve.** Let cool slightly and serve with your favorite dipping sauces. (Some great ones are sugar-free barbecue sauce, ketchup, honey mustard, buffalo sauce, or yogurt ranch.)

Note: For best results, place the nuggets directly in the air-fryer basket for proper airflow to ensure crispy nuggets.

HEALTHIER BANG BANG CHICKEN BITES

These Healthier Bang Bang Chicken Bites are an explosion of textures and flavors in every bite. They're way lower in calories than what you'd get at a restaurant, but you won't lose out on any of the flavor. The crispy chicken paired with the spicy, tangy sauce is just perfect. It's a delicious way to enjoy a restaurant favorite at home, and trust me, you won't even miss those extra calories!

Yield: Serves 4
Prep time: 25 minutes
Cook time: 12–15 minutes (Air Fryer) or 18–22 minutes (Oven)
Total time: 37–47 minutes

FOR THE CHICKEN BITES

½ cup light mayo
2 cup hot sauce
1 tbsp cornstarch
1½ lb chicken breast, cut into bite-size pieces
¾ cup cornflake breadcrumbs
¾ cup Italian breadcrumbs
1 tsp garlic powder
1 tsp onion powder
½ tsp smoked paprika
Salt and pepper, to taste
Avocado oil spray

FOR THE BANG BANG SAUCE

¼ cup plain nonfat Greek yogurt
2 tbsp light mayo
2 tbsp sweet chili sauce
1 tbsp sriracha (adjust to taste)
1 tbsp honey

1. **Preheat** the air fryer to 375°F, or the oven to 400°F.
2. **Marinate the chicken.** In a large bowl, mix together the mayo, hot sauce, and cornstarch. Add the chicken to the bowl and toss to coat evenly. Let marinate for at least 10 minutes.
3. **Prepare the coating.** In another bowl, combine the cornflake breadcrumbs, Italian breadcrumbs, garlic powder, onion powder, smoked paprika, salt, and pepper. Mix well.
4. **Coat the chicken.** Dredge each piece of marinated chicken in the breadcrumb mixture, pressing firmly to adhere.
5. **Cook the chicken.**
   Air fryer: In an air-fryer basket, arrange the breaded chicken bites in a single layer. Lightly spray with avocado oil. Air-fry for 12 to 15 minutes, flipping halfway through, until golden brown and cooked through.
   Oven: Arrange the breaded chicken bites on a wire rack placed over a baking sheet. Lightly spray with avocado oil. Bake for 18 to 22 minutes, flipping halfway through, until golden brown and crispy.
6. **Prepare the bang bang sauce.** While the chicken is cooking, in a small bowl, combine the Greek yogurt, mayo, sweet chili sauce, sriracha, and honey. Mix well.
7. **Serve.** Once the chicken bites are golden brown and crispy, remove from the air fryer or oven. Serve immediately with the bang bang sauce on the side for dipping or drizzle the sauce over the chicken bites before serving.

CHICKEN TENDERS

This was the first recipe I learned to make healthier, and it changed my life. Using this recipe, I lost 40 pounds! It made eating healthy fun and enjoyable. These chicken tenders are high in protein and lower in calories thanks to the crispy crushed-cornflakes coating and the fact that they're cooked in an air fryer instead of a deep fryer. They're deliciously crispy and perfectly seasoned, making them a crowd-pleaser while also helping you stick to your nutrition goals while enjoying every bite.

Yield: Makes 12
Prep time: 45 minutes
Cook time: 10–12 minutes (Air Fryer) or 18–22 minutes (Oven)
Total time: 55–67 minutes

1½ lb chicken breast, cut
   into ½-in strips
3 tsp Lawry's Seasoned Salt
2 tsp paprika
1 tsp granulated garlic
1 tsp onion powder
1 tsp black pepper
½ tsp cayenne pepper (optional)
1 cup all-purpose or oat flour
2 eggs, beaten
1½–2 cups cornflake breadcrumbs
Avocado oil spray

1. **Marinate the chicken.** In a large bowl, combine the chicken, seasoned salt, paprika, granulated garlic, onion powder, black pepper, and cayenne pepper (if using). Toss to coat the chicken evenly. Let marinate for at least 30 minutes.
2. **Preheat the air fryer** to 375°F, or the oven to 400°F.
3. **Dredge the chicken.** In a small bowl, add the flour. In another small bowl, add the beaten eggs. In a third small bowl, add the cornflake breadcrumbs. Coat each chicken strip in flour, then dip into the beaten eggs, and finally coat with cornflake breadcrumbs.
4. **Cook the chicken.**
   Air fryer: In the air-fryer basket, place the breaded chicken strips in a single layer. Lightly spray with avocado oil. Air-fry for 10 to 12 minutes, flipping halfway through and spraying again, until golden and cooked through to 165°F.
   Oven: Arrange the breaded chicken strips on a wire rack placed on top of a baking sheet. Lightly spray the chicken with avocado oil. Bake for 18 to 22 minutes, flipping halfway through and spraying again, until golden and cooked through to 165°F.
5. **Serve.** Serve tenders warm with my Creamy Chipotle Sauce (pg. 19), sugar-free barbecue sauce, or your favorite sauce, and enjoy!

Note: For added crispiness and flavor, replace half of the cornflake breadcrumbs with Italian breadcrumbs.

Lemon-Pepper

Garlic-Parmesan, pg. 66

LEMON-PEPPER WINGS

Buffalo Wild Wings or Wingstop? I'd easily take Buffalo Wild Wings any day, but Wingstop does have a better lemon-pepper wing. This version, though, is healthier. The wings are air-fried, making them light and crispy, and they're packed with that zesty lemon-pepper flavor. Also, boneless wings are not wings; those are chicken nuggets—don't come at me!

Yield: Serves 4
Prep time: 10 minutes
Cook time: 25–30 minutes (Air Fryer) or 45–50 minutes (Oven)
Total time: 35–60 minutes

FOR THE WINGS
2lbs chicken wings
1 tsp baking powder
1 tsp cornstarch
Avocado oil spray
1 tsp salt
1 tsp black pepper
1 tsp garlic powder
1 tsp onion powder

FOR THE LEMON-PEPPER SAUCE
2 tbsp lemon-pepper seasoning
Juice and zest of 1 lemon
2 tbsp melted butter

1. **Preheat the air fryer** to 400°F, or the oven to 425°F.
2. **Prepare the chicken wings.** Pat the chicken wings dry with paper towels. Place them in a large bowl.
3. **Mix the dry coating.** In a separate small bowl, mix together the baking powder and cornstarch. Sprinkle the mixture over the chicken wings, tossing to coat evenly.
4. **Season the wings.** Lightly spray the wings with avocado oil. In a small bowl, mix together the salt, black pepper, garlic powder, and onion powder, then sprinkle the seasonings over the wings, tossing again to coat evenly.
5. **Cook the wings.**
   Air fryer: In an air-fryer basket, arrange the wings in a single layer. Air-fry for 25 to 30 minutes, flipping the wings halfway through and spraying with avocado oil to ensure even crisping. Cook in batches to avoid overcrowding.
   Oven: On a baking sheet lined with parchment paper or on a wire rack placed on top of a baking sheet, arrange the wings in a single layer. Bake for 45 to 50 minutes, flipping the wings halfway through and spraying with avocado oil to ensure even crisping.
6. **Prepare the lemon-pepper sauce.** While the wings are cooking, in a small bowl, combine the lemon-pepper seasoning, lemon juice and zest, and melted butter. Mix well.
7. **Finish the wings.** Once the wings are golden brown and crispy, remove from the air fryer or oven. Place the cooked wings in a large bowl and pour the lemon-pepper sauce over top. Toss to coat the wings evenly.
8. **Serve.** Serve the wings immediately, accompanied by your favorite dipping sauces, such as sugar-free barbecue sauce, ketchup, honey mustard, buffalo sauce, and yogurt ranch.

GARLIC-PARMESAN WINGS

Yes, *I went there*. These Garlic-Parmesan Wings are lower in calories because they're air-fried and the sauce is made with light mayo. But don't worry, the flavors are *all there*. You can't even tell it's lower in calories. This one is a life-changer. Who knew wings could be this good and still fit into your healthy-eating plan? Get ready to be amazed and maybe a little bit obsessed!

Yield: Serves 4
Prep time: 10 minutes
Cook time: 25–30 minutes (Air Fryer) or 45–50 minutes (Oven)
Total time: 35–60 minutes

FOR THE WINGS
2lbs chicken wings
1 tsp baking powder
1 tsp cornstarch
Avocado oil spray
1 tsp salt
1 tsp pepper
1 tsp garlic powder
1 tsp onion powder
Finely chopped flat-leaf parsley,
    to garnish (optional)

FOR THE GARLIC-PARMESAN SAUCE
¼ cup light mayo
¼ cup grated Parmesan cheese
½ tsp dried thyme
½ tsp dried oregano
¼ tsp chili flakes (optional)
¼ cup plain nonfat Greek yogurt
1 tbsp lemon juice
2–3 garlic cloves, grated

1. **Preheat the air fryer** to 400°F, or the oven to 425°F.
2. **Prepare the chicken wings.** Pat the chicken wings dry with paper towels to remove any excess moisture. Place them in a large bowl.
3. **Mix the dry coating.** In a small bowl, mix together the baking powder and cornstarch. Sprinkle the mixture over the chicken wings, tossing to coat evenly.
4. **Season the wings.** Lightly spray the wings with avocado oil. In a small bowl, mix together the salt, black pepper, garlic powder, and onion powder, then sprinkle the seasonings over the wings, tossing again to coat evenly.
5. **Cook the wings.**
   Air fryer: In an air-fryer basket, arrange the wings in a single layer. Air-fry for 25 to 30 minutes, flipping the wings halfway through and spraying with avocado oil to ensure even crisping. Cook in batches to avoid overcrowding.
   Oven: On a baking sheet lined with parchment paper or on a wire rack placed on a baking sheet, arrange the wings in a single layer. Bake for 45 to 50 minutes, flipping the wings halfway through and spraying with avocado oil to ensure even crisping.
6. **Prepare the Garlic-Parmesan sauce.** While the wings are cooking, in a medium bowl, combine the light mayo, grated Parmesan cheese, dried thyme, dried oregano, chili flakes (if using), Greek yogurt, lemon juice, grated garlic, and 2 to 3 tablespoons water. Mix well until smooth. Adjust the consistency with additional water if needed.
7. **Finish the wings.** Once the wings are golden brown and crispy, remove from the air fryer or oven. Place the cooked wings in a large bowl and pour the garlic-Parmesan sauce over top. Toss to coat the wings evenly.
8. **Serve.** Serve the wings immediately, garnished with extra grated Parmesan cheese and a sprinkle of fresh parsley (if using).

BUFFALO WINGS

Growing up in Saudi Arabia, I was all about the Buffalo Wings from Fuddruckers—a US chain that's super popular in the Middle East. To this day, I still think they make the best wings. But this version? It's got all the flavor with a lighter twist. The wings are air-fried, and the sauce features a healthier take on the classic ingredients. You still get all the spicy, tangy goodness, just without the extra calories. If you love Buffalo Wings, these are a must-try!

Yield: Serves 4
Prep time: 10 minutes
Cook time: 25–30 minutes (Air Fryer) or 45–50 minutes (Oven)
Total time: 35–60 minutes

FOR THE WINGS
2lbs chicken wings
1 tsp baking powder
1 tsp cornstarch
Avocado oil spray
1 tsp salt
1 tsp black pepper
1 tsp garlic powder
1 tsp onion powder

FOR THE BUFFALO SAUCE
½ cup Frank's RedHot Buffalo Wings hot sauce
2 tbsp unsalted butter, melted

1. **Preheat the air fryer** to 400°F, or the oven to 425°F.
2. **Prepare the chicken wings.** Pat the chicken wings dry with paper towels to remove any excess moisture. Place them in a large bowl.
3. **Mix the dry coating.** In a small bowl, mix together the baking powder and cornstarch. Sprinkle the mixture over the chicken wings, tossing to coat evenly.
4. **Season the wings.** Lightly spray the wings with avocado oil. In a small bowl, mix together the salt, black pepper, garlic powder, and onion powder, then sprinkle the seasonings over the wings, tossing again to coat evenly.
5. **Cook the wings.**
    Air fryer: In an air-fryer basket, arrange the wings in a single layer. Air-fry for 25 to 30 minutes, flipping the wings halfway through and spraying with avocado oil to ensure even crisping. Cook in batches to avoid overcrowding.
    Oven: On a baking sheet lined with parchment paper or on a wire rack placed on a baking sheet, arrange the wings in a single layer. Bake for 45 to 50 minutes, flipping the wings halfway through and spraying with avocado oil to ensure even crisping.
6. **Prepare the Buffalo sauce.** While the wings are cooking, in a small bowl, combine the Frank's RedHot Sauce and melted butter. Mix well.
7. **Finish the wings.** Once the wings are golden brown and crispy, remove from the air fryer or oven. Place the cooked wings in a large bowl and pour the buffalo sauce over top. Toss to coat the wings evenly.
8. **Serve.** Serve the wings immediately, accompanied by celery sticks and blue cheese or ranch dressing.

HONEY-BARBECUE WINGS

When I was 16, my football teammates and I would go to Buffalo Wild Wings and order hundreds of wings during their "50 Cent Wings" Tuesday special. That's when I discovered how good honey-barbecue wings are. This version has all the same sweet and tangy barbecue goodness as the original but with some lower-calorie substitutions. The wings are air-fried, making them lower calorie, and the barbecue sauce is sugar-free to keep the calories down. You get all the delicious flavor without the extra calories. Dip these wings in yogurt ranch, and they are a total win!

Yield: Serves 4
Prep time: 10 minutes
Cook time: 25–30 minutes (Air Fryer) or 45–50 minutes (Oven)
Total time: 35–60 minutes

FOR THE WINGS
2lbs chicken wings
1 tsp baking powder
1 tsp cornstarch
Avocado oil spray
1 tsp salt
1 tsp black pepper
1 tsp garlic powder
1 tsp onion powder

FOR THE HONEY-BARBECUE SAUCE
1 cup of your favorite sugar-free
   barbecue sauce
2 tbsp honey
1 tbsp melted salted butter

1. **Preheat the air fryer** to 400°F, or the oven to 425°F.
2. **Prepare the chicken wings.** Pat the chicken wings dry with paper towels to remove any excess moisture. Place them in a large bowl.
3. **Mix the dry coating.** In a small bowl, mix together the baking powder and cornstarch. Sprinkle the mixture over the chicken wings, tossing to coat evenly.
4. **Season the wings.** Lightly spray the wings with avocado oil. In a small bowl, mix together the salt, black pepper, garlic powder, and onion powder, then sprinkle the seasonings over the wings, tossing again to coat evenly.
5. **Cook the wings.**
   Air fryer: In an air-fryer basket, arrange the wings in a single layer. Air-fry for 25 to 30 minutes, flipping the wings halfway through and spraying with avocado oil to ensure even crisping. Cook in batches to avoid overcrowding.
   Oven: On a baking sheet lined with parchment paper or on a wire rack placed on a baking sheet, arrange the wings in a single layer. Bake for 45 to 50 minutes, flipping the wings halfway through and spraying with avocado oil to ensure even crisping.
6. **Prepare the honey-barbecue sauce.** While the wings are cooking, in a small bowl, combine the barbecue sauce, honey, and melted butter. Mix well.
7. **Finish the wings.** Once the wings are golden brown and crispy, remove from the air fryer or oven. Place the cooked wings in a large bowl and pour the honey-barbecue sauce over top. Toss to coat the wings evenly.
8. **Serve.** Serve the wings immediately, accompanied by yogurt ranch or blue cheese dressing.

Buffalo, pg. 67

Honey-Barbeque

SIDES
SIDES
SIDES
SIDES
SIDES
SIDES
SIDES

Naturally sweet, perfectly crispy, and totally addictive.

SWEET POTATO FRIES WITH LOW-CALORIE CHIPOTLE AIOLI

When I was 18, I worked at a restaurant called G Burger, where I fell in love with sweet potato fries dipped in the house-made aioli. This recipe is an homage to that dish but healthier. The combination of sweet, salty, crunchy, spicy, and smoky flavors will blow your socks off. The sweet potato fries are air-fried to perfection, and the low-calorie chipotle aioli adds a delicious kick.

Yield: Serves 4
Prep time: 15 minutes
Cook time: 13–16 minutes (Air Fryer) or 19–23 minutes (Oven)
Total time: 28–38 minutes

FOR THE SWEET POTATO FRIES

2 large sweet potatoes, peeled and cut into ½-in strips
1 tbsp cornstarch or arrowroot starch
1 tbsp olive oil or avocado oil
½ tsp salt
1 tsp garlic powder (optional)

FOR THE LOW-CALORIE CHIPOTLE AIOLI

¼ cup plain nonfat Greek yogurt
2 tbsp light mayo
1–2 chipotle peppers in adobo sauce, finely chopped (adjust to taste)
1 tsp adobo sauce from the can
1 tsp lime juice
½ tsp garlic powder
Salt and pepper, to taste

1. **Preheat the air fryer** to 375°F, or the oven to 400°F.
2. **Prepare the sweet potato fries.** In a large bowl, toss the sweet potato strips with the cornstarch until evenly coated. This helps to make the fries crispy. Drizzle the olive oil over the sweet potatoes. In a separate small bowl, mix together the salt and garlic powder (if using). Sprinkle the seasoning mix over the sweet potatoes and toss to coat evenly.
3. **Cook the fries.**
   Air fryer: In an air-fryer basket, arrange the sweet potato fries in a single layer. Air-fry for 13 to 16 minutes, shaking the basket halfway through to ensure even crisping.
   Oven: On a baking sheet lined with parchment paper, spread the sweet potato fries in a single layer. Bake for 19 to 23 minutes, flipping halfway through to ensure even crisping.
4. **Prepare the chipotle aioli.** While the fries are cooking, in a small bowl, combine the Greek yogurt, light mayo, chipotle peppers, adobo sauce, lime juice, garlic powder, salt, and pepper. Mix well until smooth and adjust the seasoning to taste.
5. **Serve.** Once the sweet potato fries are golden brown and crispy, remove from the air fryer or oven. Serve immediately with the low-calorie chipotle aioli on the side for dipping.

HOMEMADE FAST-FOOD FRIES

These Homemade Fast-Food Fries will blow you away with how good they taste. Seriously, they're so similar to the real deal but without being deep-fried. You can eat a whole bowl of these for the same calories as a small-fry order from your favorite fast-food joint. They're crispy, flavorful, and super easy to make. Trust me, once you try these, you won't miss the drive-thru fries at all!

Yield: Serves 4
Prep time: 40 minutes
Cook time: 20–25 minutes (Air Fryer) or 30–35 minutes (Oven)
Total time: 60–75 minutes

4 large Russet potatoes,
   cut into ¼-in strips
2 tbsp avocado oil
1 tsp salt
½ tsp garlic powder (optional)
½ tsp paprika (optional)
½ tsp onion powder (optional)

1. **Preheat the air fryer** to 375°F, or the oven to 425°F.
2. **Prepare the potatoes.** In a bowl of cold water, place the potato strips. Soak for at least 30 minutes to remove excess starch and help the fries crisp up. (If you're short on time, this step is optional, but your fries won't turn out as crispy without it.) Drain the potatoes and pat dry thoroughly with paper towels.
3. **Season the potatoes.** In a large bowl, combine the potatoes with the avocado oil and salt. Add the garlic powder, paprika, and onion powder (if using) for enhanced flavor.
4. **Cook the potatoes.**
   Air fryer: In the air-fryer basket, arrange the potato strips in a single layer. Air-fry for 20 to 25 minutes, gently flipping the fries halfway through for even crisping. Cook in batches to avoid overcrowding
   Oven: On a baking sheet lined with parchment paper, spread out the potato strips in a single layer. Bake for 30 to 35 minutes, gently flipping the fries halfway through for even crisping.
5. **Season and serve.** Once the fries are golden brown and crispy, remove from the air fryer or oven. Sprinkle with additional salt or other seasonings, if desired. Serve the fries immediately with your favorite dipping sauces, such as ketchup, mayo, or my Low-Calorie Chipotle Aioli included with the Sweet Potato Fries recipe (pg. 73).

MEXICAN-INSPIRED LOADED BAKED POTATO

Growing up in California, I was surrounded by incredible Mexican food, and this Mexican-Inspired Loaded Baked Potato brings back all those flavors. It's packed with seasoned ground beef, melted cheese, salsa, and a dollop of Greek yogurt. It's a healthier, high-protein twist on a classic comfort food, and it's perfect for when you're craving those bold Mexican flavors without all the extra calories. Seriously, it's like a fiesta in every bite!

Yield: Makes 4
Prep time: 10 minutes
Cook time: 1 hour
Total time: 1 hour 10 minutes

4 large Russet potatoes
2–3 tbsp olive oil
1lb lean ground beef
1–2 tbsp taco seasoning
1 cup shredded low-fat
   Mexican-blend cheese
½ cup plain nonfat Greek
   yogurt or light sour cream
½ cup salsa
1 avocado, sliced (optional)
¼ cup chopped green onions
¼ cup chopped fresh cilantro
   (optional)
Salt and pepper, to taste

1. **Preheat the oven** to 400°F.
2. **Prepare the potatoes.** Scrub the potatoes clean and pat dry with a cloth or paper towel. With a fork, pierce each potato several times, brush them with 1 to 2 teaspoons of olive oil each, and sprinkle with salt.
3. **Bake the potatoes.** Place the potatoes directly on the oven rack or on a lined baking sheet. Bake for about 60 minutes, or until the potatoes are fork-tender.
4. **Prepare the toppings.** While the potatoes are baking, heat a large skillet over medium-high heat. Add the ground beef and taco seasoning, and cook until browned and cooked through. Add ¼ cup of water to deglaze the skillet for the last 2 to 3 minutes of cooking the beef. Remove from the heat and set aside.
5. **Cut and fluff the potatoes.** Once the potatoes are done, remove from the oven and set aside to cool for a few minutes. After the potatoes have rested, cut a slit down the center of each potato and fluff the insides with a fork.
6. **Add the toppings and serve.** Top each potato with the seasoned ground beef, shredded cheese, a dollop of Greek yogurt, salsa, and avocado slices (if using). Garnish with the green onions and cilantro (if using). Season with salt and pepper to taste and enjoy.

CRISPY ONION RINGS

I first fell in love with onion rings as a kid growing up in Saudi Arabia. I'd always order them from Burger King. This healthier version has all the crunch and amazing flavor I remember, but it's lighter because they're air-fried. These onion rings are crispy, delicious, and perfect for dipping in yogurt ranch or sugar-free barbecue sauce. Trust me, you won't even miss the deep-fried version!

Yield: Serves 4
Prep time: 15 minutes
Cook time: 10–15 minutes (Air Fryer) or 15–20 minutes (Oven)
Total time: 25–35 minutes

1 cup all-purpose or
    whole wheat flour
2 tsp baking powder
1 tsp salt
2 tsp paprika (optional)
2 tsp garlic powder (optional)
2 tsp onion powder (optional)
1 tsp black pepper (optional)
1 cup light beer or sparkling water
3 cups cornflake breadcrumbs
3 cups Italian breadcrumbs
2 large onions, sliced into rings
Avocado oil spray

1. **Preheat the air fryer** to 400°F, or the oven to 425°F.
2. **Prepare the batter.** In a large bowl, mix together the flour, baking powder, salt and the paprika, garlic powder, onion powder, and black pepper (if using). Add the light beer and whisk until smooth.
3. **Coat the onion rings.** In a separate shallow bowl, mix together the cornflake breadcrumbs and the Italian breadcrumbs. Dip the onion rings into the batter one at a time, ensuring they're fully coated. Then, coat each ring with the breadcrumb mixture, pressing firmly to adhere. Spray 8 to 10 times with avocado oil.
4. **Cook the onion rings.**
   Air fryer: In an air-fryer basket, arrange the breaded onion rings in a single layer. Air-fry for 10 to 15 minutes, monitoring closely to make sure they don't burn.
   Oven: On a baking sheet lined with parchment paper, arrange the breaded onion rings in a single layer. Bake for 15 to 20 minutes, gently flipping halfway through and spraying with more avocado oil for even crisping. Monitor the onion rings closely to make sure they don't burn.
5. **Serve.** Once the onion rings are golden brown and crispy, remove them from the air fryer or oven and serve immediately with your favorite dipping sauce.

Crispy Onion Rings

Healthier Caesar Salad with Yogurt Dressing

HEALTHIER CAESAR SALAD WITH YOGURT DRESSING

As a kid, I always ordered Caesar salads whenever my family went out to eat—it was my first intro to "salads." This healthier version is a cleaner, better-for-you twist with a yogurt-based dressing. It's just as creamy and delicious as the classic, but you'll feel great enjoying it. The tangy yogurt dressing pairs perfectly with the crisp romaine and savory Parmesan. If you're a Caesar-salad lover, this is a must-try!

Yield: Serves 4
Prep time: 15 minutes
Cook time: 0 minutes
Total time: 15 minutes

⅓ cup plain low-fat or nonfat
   Greek yogurt
2 anchovy fillets, mashed
1 garlic clove, minced
2 tbsp lemon juice
2 tsp Worcestershire sauce
2 tbsp extra-virgin olive oil
¼ cup freshly grated
   Parmigiano-Reggiano
   cheese, divided
1 tsp black pepper
Kosher salt, to taste
1 large head of romaine lettuce,
   torn into bite-size pieces

1. **Prepare the dressing.** In a small bowl, combine the Greek yogurt, mashed anchovy fillets, garlic, lemon juice, and Worcestershire sauce. Whisk together until well blended.
2. **Add the oil.** Slowly whisk in the extra-virgin olive oil to create a smooth emulsion.
3. **Add the cheese and seasonings.** Stir half of the grated Parmigiano-Reggiano cheese into the dressing. Season with the black pepper and kosher salt to taste.
4. **Dress the salad.** In a large salad bowl, add the torn romaine lettuce. Pour the dressing over the lettuce. Toss well to evenly coat.
5. **Garnish and serve.** Sprinkle the remaining Parmigiano-Reggiano cheese over the salad. Divide the salad evenly among plates or bowls, serve immediately and enjoy!

CRISPY SMASHED POTATO SALAD

When I posted my Crispy Smashed Potato Salad recipe in October 2023, it went viral, and everyone and their grandmas started making it. But here's the secret: I didn't actually invent the dish. I was inspired by a restaurant called JOEY in Newport Beach, California. Their cajun blackened chicken came with a side of warm potato salad that was crunchy, creamy, and packed with flavor. I had to recreate it, and it became a trend. I'm pretty sure I was the first to share it on social media though. So technically, I started the trend, right?

Yield: Serves 4
Prep time: 5 minutes
Cook time: 45–60 minutes
Total time: 50–65 minutes

FOR THE SMASHED POTATOES

2 tbsp avocado oil, divided
3lbs baby potatoes, scrubbed
Salt and pepper, to taste

FOR THE SALAD

¾ cup plain low-fat or nonfat
  Greek yogurt
½ cup light mayo
2 tsp Dijon mustard
Juice of ½ large lemon
2 tsp red wine vinegar
1–2 garlic cloves, minced
¼ cup chopped fresh dill
¼ cup chopped fresh parsley
1 medium stalk celery, finely
  chopped
1 shallot, finely chopped
3–4 cooked crispy bacon strips,
  crumbled

1. **Preheat the oven** to 400°F. Grease a baking sheet with 1 tablespoon of the avocado oil.
2. **Cook the potatoes.** Bring a large pot of salted water to a boil, then add the baby potatoes. Boil until the potatoes are fork-tender, 15 to 20 minutes. Drain and let dry for a minute.
3. **Smash the potatoes.** On the greased baking sheet, place the potatoes, then use a potato masher or the bottom of a cup to smash each potato to about ½-inch thickness. Brush the potatoes with ½ tablespoon of avocado oil and season with salt and pepper.
4. **Bake the potatoes.** Bake for about 30 to 40 minutes until the edges are crispy and golden brown. Flip the potatoes every 10 to 15 minutes and rebrush with ½ tablespoon of avocado oil, if desired.
5. **Prepare the salad dressing.** While the potatoes are baking, in a large bowl, combine the Greek yogurt, mayo, Dijon mustard, lemon juice, red wine vinegar, garlic, dill, and parsley. Stir well to blend. Add the celery and shallot to the dressing and mix thoroughly.
6. **Dress the potatoes.** Once the potatoes are crispy, remove from the oven and let cool slightly. Add the smashed potatoes to the dressing right before serving to ensure the potatoes remain crispy. (They might become soggy if they sit too long in the dressing.) Gently toss until the potatoes are evenly coated with the dressing and top with the crumbled bacon.
7. **Serve.** Serve the salad warm or at room temperature.

Note: If using a stainless steel baking sheet, feel free to use a spatula to scrape the potatoes off when flipping to get that nice crust.

Crispy, creamy, and so satisfying!

COPYCAT CHICK-FIL-A SOUTHWEST SALAD WITH CREAMY SALSA DRESSING

The Chick-fil-A Spicy Southwest Salad is my absolute favorite, but eating out every week can really add up. Making a bigger portion at home is a great way to enjoy it without breaking the bank. Plus, you get all the deliciousness of the spicy grilled chicken, the fresh veggies, and the amazing creamy salsa dressing. It's satisfying, flavorful, and perfect for meal prepping too. Now I can indulge in my favorite salad whenever I want and save some money!

Yield: Serves 4
Prep time: 20 minutes
Cook time: 15 minutes
Total time: 35 minutes

FOR THE CHICKEN MARINADE

1 tbsp olive oil

1 tsp chili powder

1 tsp cumin

½ tsp smoked paprika

½ tsp garlic powder (optional)

½ tsp onion powder (optional)

¼ tsp cayenne pepper (optional)

Salt and pepper, to taste

1 lb boneless, skinless
   chicken breasts

FOR THE CREAMY SALSA DRESSING

½ cup plain nonfat Greek yogurt

¼ cup light sour cream

¼ cup salsa (your favorite brand)

1 tbsp lime juice

½ tsp cumin

½ tsp chili powder

Salt and pepper, to taste

FOR THE SALAD

6 cups mixed greens (romaine,
   kale, and spring mix)

1½ cups halved grape tomatoes

¾ cup black beans, drained
   and rinsed

¾ cup roasted corn, drained

½ cup diced poblano chiles

½ cup diced red bell pepper

½ cup shredded low-fat Monterey
   Jack and cheddar cheese blend

½ cup seasoned tortilla strips

½ cup chili-lime pepitas
   (pumpkin seeds)

1½ avocados, sliced,
   to garnish (optional)

recipe continues on pg. 88

COPYCAT CHICK-FIL-A SOUTHWEST SALAD WITH CREAMY SALSA DRESSING

continued from pg. 87

1. **Marinate the chicken.** In a small bowl, mix together the olive oil, chili powder, cumin, and smoked paprika; the garlic powder, onion powder, and cayenne pepper (if using); and the salt and pepper. Rub the mixture all over the chicken breasts. Allow the chicken to marinate while you preheat the grill or a skillet over medium-high heat.
2. **Cook the chicken.** To the hot grill or skillet, add the marinated chicken breasts. Grill or cook for 6 to 8 minutes per side, or until the internal temperature of each breast reaches 165°F. Ensure the chicken is nicely seared and cooked through. Remove from the heat and let rest for a few minutes.
3. **Prepare the dressing.** While the chicken rests, in a medium bowl, whisk together the Greek yogurt, sour cream, salsa, lime juice, cumin, chili powder, salt, and pepper until smooth. Adjust the seasoning to taste. Set aside.
4. **Assemble the salad.** In a large bowl or on individual serving plates, arrange the mixed greens. Top with the grape tomatoes, black beans, roasted corn, poblano chiles, bell pepper, shredded cheese, tortilla strips, and chili-lime pepitas. Add the avocado slices (if using).
5. **Add the chicken.** Slice the cooked chicken breasts and place them on top of the salad.
6. **Serve with the dressing.** Drizzle the creamy salsa dressing over the salad or serve it on the side.

Note: To meal prep this salad for the week, store the mixed greens, chicken, and salad toppings in separate airtight containers and keep the creamy salsa dressing in a small container on the side. Assemble the salad just before eating to ensure the greens stay crisp and fresh.

AIR-FRIED CHIPS

When I was a kid, I used to eat a ton of chips—who didn't, right? Now, this air-fried version is a total lifesaver because they're lower in calories, so you can munch on more and still feel good about it. They're crispy, delicious, and have the perfect crunch when you're craving a savory snack. Honestly, these chips are perfect for anyone who loves snacking but wants to keep their health goals in check.

Yield: Serves 4
Prep time: 15 minutes
Cook time: 25 minutes
Total time: 40 minutes

4 medium yellow potatoes,
   peeled and sliced to ¼ in thick
1 tbsp avocado oil
Salt, to taste

1. **Prep the potatoes.** In a bowl of cold water, place the sliced potatoes. Soak for at least 10 minutes to remove excess starch and make the fries crispier. Then, drain the water, and using a clean kitchen towel or paper towels, pat the potato slices dry to remove as much moisture as possible.
2. **Preheat the air fryer** to 380°F.
3. **Season the potatoes.** Transfer the potato slices to a clean, dry bowl. Drizzle with the avocado oil and toss to coat evenly. Sprinkle salt over the chips and toss again to distribute evenly.
4. **Cook the chips.** In an air-fryer basket, arrange the potato slices in a single layer. Cook in batches to avoid overcrowding if necessary. Air-fry for 20 to 25 minutes. Halfway through, shake the basket or use tongs to flip the chips so they get crispy on all sides.
5. **Adjust the seasoning.** Taste a chip immediately after cooking, and if needed, adjust the salt while they are still hot.
6. **Serve.** Serve the chips hot and crispy, straight from the air fryer.

BIG MAC SALAD

The Big Mac has been my go-to at McDonald's since I first tasted one at eight years old. But let's be real, that middle bun is totally pointless. This Big Mac salad has all the elements of the classic burger but is low-calorie so you can eat a huge bowl of it and still stick to your health goals. It's got the juicy beef, special sauce, and all the fixings you love. Trust me, ditch the bun and dive straight into this—you'll love it!

Yield: Serves 4
Prep time: 10 minutes
Cook time: 10 minutes
Total time: 20 minutes

FOR THE BIG MAC SAUCE

3/4 cup light mayo

3/4 cup plain nonfat Greek yogurt

3 tbsp sweet pickle relish

1 tbsp grated white onion

1 tbsp yellow mustard

1 tsp honey

1/2 tsp paprika

1/2 tsp onion powder

1/2 tsp fine sea salt

1/2 tsp garlic powder

FOR THE SALAD

1lb lean ground beef

Salt and pepper, to taste

1 tsp garlic powder

1 tsp onion powder

4 cups shredded iceberg lettuce

1/4 cup finely chopped white onion

1/4 cup finely chopped dill pickles

1/4 cup shredded low-fat Mexican-blend cheese

Sesame seeds, to garnish

1. **Prepare the Big Mac sauce.** In a small bowl, combine the mayo, Greek yogurt, relish, onion, mustard, honey, paprika, onion powder, sea salt, and garlic powder. Whisk until well blended and smooth.

2. **Cook the beef.** Heat a large skillet over medium-high heat for 3 to 5 minutes. Add the ground beef, breaking it up with a spatula. Season with the salt, pepper, garlic powder, and onion powder. Cook for 4 to 6 minutes or until the beef is browned and no longer pink. Remove from the heat and set aside to cool slightly.

3. **Assemble the salad.** In a large bowl, toss the shredded iceberg lettuce with the onions, pickles, cooled ground beef, and shredded cheese. Drizzle the Big Mac sauce over top and toss again to coat evenly.

4. **Garnish and serve.** Sprinkle the sesame seeds over the salad, then serve fresh.

All the Big Mac vibes, without the bun!

CHINESE TAKEOUT FRIED RICE

My obsession with Chinese food began at a young age, when I was growing up in Saudi Arabia. My family and I would go out to eat Chinese food almost every weekend. Fried rice became one of my favorites, and I especially ate it a lot when I was overweight—I seriously loved it. This version is packed with protein and tastes even better. It's got all the good stuff in it—crispy rice, juicy chicken, and fresh veggies. Plus, it's perfect for meal prep, so you can enjoy it throughout the week. Trust me, you'll love this just as much as the takeout version, if not more!

Yield: Serves 4
Prep time: 15 minutes
Cook time: 20 minutes
Total time: 35 minutes

3 tsp avocado oil, divided

1lb boneless, skinless chicken breasts, diced

Salt and pepper, to taste

1 small onion, diced

2 garlic cloves, minced

1 tsp minced ginger

1 cup frozen peas and carrots

1 red bell pepper, diced

1 cup egg whites (or 4 large eggs, beaten)

2 cups cooked day-old short-grain or long-grain white rice

1 tbsp low-sodium soy sauce

1 tbsp oyster sauce (optional)

2 tbsp low-sodium chicken broth or water (if needed)

1 tsp sesame oil

Sliced green onions, for garnish

1. **Cook the chicken.** Heat a nonstick skillet or wok over medium-high heat. Add 1 teaspoon of the avocado oil, then the chicken. Season with salt and pepper and cook until the chicken is no longer pink and is cooked through to 165°F. Remove from the skillet and set aside.

2. **Cook the vegetables.** To the same skillet, add another 1 teaspoon of the avocado oil. Add the onion, garlic, and ginger. Sauté for 2 to 3 minutes, until fragrant. Add the frozen peas and carrots and the bell pepper. Cook for another 3 to 4 minutes, until the vegetables are tender.

3. **Cook the eggs.** Push the vegetables to one side of the skillet. Pour the egg whites or beaten eggs into the skillet on the opposite side. Scramble the eggs until fully cooked, then mix them in with the vegetables.

4. **Combine the ingredients.** To the skillet, add the cooked white rice and cooked chicken. Stir everything together until well combined. Add the soy sauce and oyster sauce (if using). If the mixture seems too dry, add a bit of chicken broth or water.

5. **Crisp up the rice.** Push the rice mixture to one side of the skillet and add the remaining 1 teaspoon of avocado oil to the empty side. Spread the rice mixture over the entire skillet and let it cook undisturbed for 2 to 3 minutes to crisp up the rice. Stir and repeat once more for even crispiness. Add the sesame oil at the very end and stir through for added flavor and crispiness.

6. **Season, garnish, and serve.** Taste the fried rice and adjust the seasoning with salt and pepper if needed. Garnish with sliced green onions and serve immediately.

Storage and Reheating Instructions: Divide the fried rice into airtight containers and refrigerate for up to 4 days. Reheat in a skillet over medium heat or in the microwave, adding a splash of water or soy sauce to revive the texture and flavor.

HANDHELDS
HANDHELDS
HANDHELDS
HANDHELDS
HANDHELDS
HANDHELDS
HANDHELDS

HIGH-PROTEIN, LOW-CALORIE GRINDER SANDWICH

The High-Protein, Low-Calorie Grinder Sandwich is an amazing way to savor bold, delicious flavors while still keeping things healthy. I love how you can enjoy the viral trends you see online but with a healthier twist. This sandwich has all the same mouthwatering flavors as a typical grinder but is packed with high-protein ingredients and fresh veggies so you can feel great about every bite. It's the perfect example of how you can enjoy a hearty, satisfying meal and stay on track with your nutritional goals.

Yield: Makes 4
Prep time: 20 minutes
Cook time: 15 minutes
Total time: 35 minutes

FOR THE CHICKEN
1 tbsp olive oil
1 tsp garlic powder
1 tsp onion powder
½ tsp smoked paprika
1 tsp salt
½ tsp black pepper
1lb boneless, skinless chicken breasts

FOR THE GRINDER SALAD
2 cups shredded lettuce
½ cup halved cherry tomatoes
¼ cup thinly sliced red onion
¼ cup sliced pepperoncini
¼ cup light mayo
¼ cup plain nonfat Greek yogurt
1 tbsp red wine vinegar
1 tsp oregano
½ tsp garlic powder
½ tsp onion powder
Salt and pepper, to taste

FOR THE SANDWICH
2 whole wheat hoagie rolls or low-carb sandwich rolls
2 slices low-fat provolone or mozzarella cheese
½ avocado, sliced (optional)

1. **Preheat the oven** to 350°F. At the same time, preheat a grill or skillet over medium-high heat.
2. **Prepare the chicken.** In a small bowl, mix together the olive oil, garlic powder, onion powder, smoked paprika, salt, and pepper. Rub the mixture all over the chicken breasts. Grill or cook the chicken breasts for 5 to 7 minutes per side, or until the internal temperature reaches 165°F. Remove from the heat and let rest for a few minutes, then slice.
3. **Prepare the grinder salad.** In a large bowl, combine the lettuce, cherry tomatoes, red onion, and pepperoncini. In a separate small bowl, whisk together the mayo, Greek yogurt, red wine vinegar, oregano, garlic powder, onion powder, salt, and pepper. Pour the dressing over the salad and toss to combine.
4. **Assemble the sandwich.** Slice the hoagie rolls in half lengthwise and place a slice of cheese inside each roll. Toast in the oven for about 5 minutes, or until the cheese is melted.
5. **Add the fillings.** Place the chicken breast slices inside each hoagie roll. Top with a generous amount of grinder salad. Add the avocado (if using).
6. **Serve.** Cut the sandwiches in half and serve immediately.

HEALTHIER COPYCAT POPEYES CHICKEN SANDWICH

Which is better, Popeyes or KFC? We all know the answer is Popeyes, and what I love about this recipe is that even though it's a healthier version of their chicken sandwich with fewer calories, you still feel like you're eating Popeyes. It has all the crunch and flavor of the original. The secret is in the marinade and in the perfect mix of flour, cornstarch, and cornflakes breadcrumbs for that crispy coating.

Yield: Makes 2
Prep time: 45 minutes
Cook time: 12–15 minutes (Air Fryer) or 20–25 minutes (Oven)
Total time: 57–70 minutes

FOR THE CHICKEN
1 egg white
1 tbsp cornstarch
1 tsp garlic powder
1 tsp onion powder
Salt and pepper, to taste
¼ cup pickle juice
½ tsp cayenne pepper (optional)
2 (8oz) boneless, skinless
  chicken breasts
Cooking spray

FOR THE DREDGING
⅓ cup flour
⅓ cup cornstarch
⅓ cup cornflakes breadcrumbs

FOR ASSEMBLY
2 brioche buns
Pickles
Light mayo or yogurt-based sauce

1. **Marinate the chicken.** In a medium bowl, mix together the egg white, cornstarch, garlic powder, onion powder, salt, pepper, pickle juice, and cayenne pepper (if using). Add the chicken breasts and let marinate for at least 30 minutes in the fridge.
2. **Preheat the air fryer** to 375°F, or the oven to 400°F.
3. **Prepare the dredge.** In medium shallow bowl, combine the flour, cornstarch, and cornflakes breadcrumbs.
4. **Coat the chicken.** Remove the chicken from the marinade. Coat each breast in the dredge mixture, pressing firmly to ensure it adheres well. Lightly spray the chicken with cooking spray.
5. **Cook the chicken.**
   Air fryer: In an air-fryer basket, place the breaded chicken. Air-fry for 12 to 15 minutes, flipping halfway through, until golden and cooked through to 165°F.
   Oven: On a baking sheet lined with parchment paper, place the breaded chicken. Bake for 20 to 25 minutes, flipping halfway through, until golden and cooked through to 165°F.
6. **Assemble the sandwich.** Toast your brioche buns, add your favorite toppings (like pickles and a light mayo or yogurt-based sauce), and enjoy!

Crispy, juicy, and serving main character energy!

LOW-CALORIE COPYCAT CHICKEN SNACK WRAP

The McDonald's Chicken Snack Wrap was a childhood favorite of mine, and I was heartbroken when they discontinued it. So, I had to recreate it with this recipe. It's lower in calories but still tastes amazing—just like the original. The combination of crispy chicken, fresh lettuce, and tangy sauce wrapped in a tortilla brings back so many good memories.

Yield: Makes 4
Prep time: 1 hour
Cook time: 15 minutes
Total time: 1 hour 15 minutes

FOR THE CHICKEN MARINADE

1lb boneless, skinless chicken breasts or thighs, cut into strips
1 cup low-fat buttermilk
2 tbsp pickle juice
1 tbsp hot sauce
1 tsp garlic powder (optional)
1 tsp onion powder (optional)
Salt and pepper, to taste

FOR THE DREDGING

2 eggs, beaten
½ cup oat or all-purpose flour
1 cup cornflake breadcrumbs or crushed protein chips
Olive oil spray
½ tsp salt
¼ tsp pepper

FOR THE SAUCE

¼ cup plain nonfat Greek yogurt
¼ cup light mayo
Squeeze of lemon juice
¼ tsp lemon zest
Salt, to taste
1 tsp black pepper

TO SERVE

4 large low-carb or whole wheat tortillas
½ cup shredded low-fat cheddar cheese
1 cup shredded lettuce
½ cup diced tomatoes

1. **Marinate the chicken.** In a medium bowl, combine the chicken, buttermilk, pickle juice, hot sauce, garlic powder and onion powder (if using), salt, and pepper. Cover and refrigerate for at least 30 minutes to tenderize the chicken and enhance the flavor.
2. **Preheat the oven** to 425°F.
3. **Set up the dredging station.** In 3 separate shallow dishes, place the beaten eggs, oat flour, and cornflake breadcrumbs. Season the oat flour with salt and pepper.
4. **Coat the chicken.** Remove the chicken from the marinade, allowing excess liquid to drip off. Dredge each strip of chicken in the oat flour first, then in the beaten eggs, and finally in the cornflake breadcrumbs, pressing firmly to adhere. Lightly spray with olive oil.
5. **Cook the chicken.** On a baking sheet lined with parchment paper, arrange the breaded chicken strips in a single layer. Bake for 15 minutes, flipping halfway through, until the chicken is crispy and cooked through.
6. **Make the sauce.** While the chicken is cooking, in a small bowl, mix together the Greek yogurt and mayo. Add a squeeze of lemon juice, the lemon zest, salt to taste, and the black pepper. Stir until well combined.
7. **Warm the tortillas.** Warm the tortillas in a dry skillet over medium heat, or in the microwave, until pliable.
8. **Assemble the wraps.** Lay each tortilla flat on a clean workspace. Place a few chicken strips in the center of each tortilla. Sprinkle with shredded cheese, lettuce, and tomatoes. Add a dollop of the prepared sauce over top.
9. **Wrap.** Fold the sides of the tortilla over the filling, then roll it up tightly from the bottom. Serve immediately.

HEALTHIER COPYCAT CHICK-FIL-A CHICKEN SANDWICH

I immigrated to the United States when I was 12, and the first time I tried Chick-fil-A, it left me in a daze. How could a chicken sandwich taste *that good*? It quickly became one of my favorites, and I used to hit up Chick-fil-A all the time after football practice—it's a classic! This recipe really nails the taste, but it's a healthier version since there's no deep-frying involved. The cornflakes give the chicken that perfect crunch, just like the original, so you can enjoy it while keeping things lighter and healthier.

Yield: Makes 4

Prep time: 1 hour 15 minutes (or longer, for additional marinating time)

Cook time: 10–12 minutes (Air Fryer) or 15–20 minutes (Oven)

Total time: 1 hour 30 minutes

FOR THE CHICKEN MARINADE

½ cup pickle juice
¼ cup buttermilk
1 tbsp hot sauce
1 tsp garlic powder (optional)
1 tsp onion powder (optional)
¾ tsp salt
½ tsp black pepper
2 boneless, skinless chicken breasts (sliced in half crosswise to make 4 thin fillets)

FOR THE DREDGING

½ cup all-purpose or oat flour
2 eggs, beaten
1 cup cornflakes breadcrumbs

TO COOK AND SERVE

Cooking spray
4 St. Pierre Brioche Burger Buns or low-carb buns
Lettuce leaves
Sliced tomatoes
Sliced dill pickles

1. **Marinate the chicken.** In a bowl, combine the pickle juice, buttermilk, hot sauce, garlic and onion powder (if using), salt, and pepper. Add the chicken fillets and ensure they are fully submerged. Marinate in the refrigerator for at least 1 hour, preferably overnight.

2. **Preheat the oven** to 400°F, or the air fryer to 375°F.

3. **Set up the dredging station.** Gather 3 small bowls for the dredging process. In the first bowl, place the flour. In the second, add the beaten eggs. In the third, place the cornflakes breadcrumbs.

4. **Bread the chicken.** Working 1 fillet at a time, remove the chicken from the marinade and let any excess drip off. First dredge each fillet in flour, then dip in the beaten eggs, and finally coat with the cornflakes breadcrumbs. Lightly spray the fillets with cooking spray.

5. **Cook the chicken.**
Air fryer: In an air-fryer basket, place the breaded chicken fillets in a single layer. Air-fry for 10 to 12 minutes, flipping halfway through, until the chicken is golden and cooked through to 165°F.
Oven: On a baking sheet lined with parchment paper, place the breaded chicken fillets so they aren't touching. Bake for 15 to 20 minutes, flipping halfway through, until the chicken is golden and cooked through to 165°F.

6. **Assemble the sandwiches.** Toast the buns. Place a lettuce leaf and slice of tomato on the bottom bun, add the cooked chicken fillet over top, then add the pickles and the top bun. Serve immediately.

CHICKEN SHAWARMA WRAP

Growing up with a Lebanese heritage, shawarma has always been a staple in my life. This recipe brings back those cherished memories with its simple yet exquisite flavors. I love how this dish captures the essence of traditional shawarma, combining marinated chicken with fresh ingredients and my mom's famous Garlicky White Sauce. It's a delightful and healthy way to enjoy a taste of my childhood, perfect for anyone looking to savor authentic Lebanese cuisine in a straightforward, delicious meal.

Yield: Makes 4
Prep time: 1 hour 15 minutes (or longer, for additional marinating time)
Cook time: 15 minutes
Total time: 1 hour 30 minutes

FOR THE CHICKEN MARINADE
2 tbsp olive oil
Juice of 1 lemon
3 garlic cloves, minced
1 tsp ground cumin
1 tsp ground allspice
1 tsp paprika
½ tsp turmeric
½ tsp ground cinnamon
1 tsp salt
½ tsp pepper
1½lbs boneless, skinless chicken thighs

FOR THE WRAP
4 low-carb tortillas
Homemade Fast-Food Fries (pg. 74) or frozen fries, according to package instructions
Arabic pickles, sliced
Garlicky White Sauce (pg. 19)

1. **Marinate the chicken.** In a large bowl, combine the olive oil, lemon juice, garlic, cumin, allspice, paprika, turmeric, cinnamon, salt, and pepper. Add the chicken thighs and coat them thoroughly with the marinade. Cover and refrigerate for at least 1 hour, preferably overnight, to allow the flavors to penetrate the meat.

2. **Cook the chicken.** Preheat the grill or a skillet over medium-high heat. Cook the marinated chicken thighs for 5 to 7 minutes per side, or until nicely charred on the outside and fully cooked through to 165°F. Remove from the heat and let the chicken rest for a few minutes, then slice into thin strips.

3. **Assemble the wraps.** Warm the tortillas on a skillet over medium heat, or in the microwave, until they are pliable. Place a handful of crispy air-fried fries in the center of each tortilla. Add slices of the chicken shawarma on top. Add Arabic pickles and drizzle generously with the garlic sauce.

4. **Wrap and serve.** Fold the sides of the tortilla over the filling, then roll it up tightly from the bottom. Serve the wraps immediately while still warm so the flavors are at their peak.

All the Cali vibes, wrapped and ready to roll!

LOWER-CALORIE CALIFORNIA BURRITO

The California burrito is a dish close to my heart, as I grew up in California after moving from the Middle East when I was 12. This burrito brings back memories of high school and beach days with friends. While traditional California burritos are delicious, they're often high in calories. This version is lower in calories and packed with protein, making it a healthier option without compromising on flavor. The combination of juicy flank steak, crispy air-fried fries, Greek yogurt in place of sour cream, and other fresh toppings makes it a nostalgic and satisfying meal.

Yield: Makes 4
Prep time: 1 hour 30 minutes (or longer, for additional marinating time)
Cook time: 25–30 minutes
Total time: 2 hours

FOR THE FLANK STEAK MARINADE

2 tbsp olive oil
Juice of 1 lime
3 garlic cloves, minced
1 tsp ground cumin
1 tsp chili powder
Salt and pepper, to taste
1 lb flank steak

FOR THE FRENCH FRIES & ASSEMBLY

Homemade Fast-Food Fries (pg. 74) or frozen fries, according to package instructions
4 large whole wheat or low-carb tortillas
½ cup shredded low-fat cheddar cheese
½ cup plain nonfat Greek yogurt
½ cup fresh salsa
1 avocado, sliced

1. **Marinate the flank steak.** In a small bowl, combine the olive oil, lime juice, garlic, cumin, chili powder, salt, and pepper and mix well. In a resealable bag or shallow dish, place the flank steak and pour the marinade over top. Marinate in the refrigerator for at least 1 hour, preferably overnight.

2. **Preheat the air fryer** to 385°F. At the same time, preheat a grill or skillet over medium-high heat.

3. **Make the french fries.** Follow the instructions for the Homemade Fast-Food Fries, or use frozen french fries and prepare them according to package instructions.

4. **Cook the flank steak.** Remove the steak from the marinade and pat it dry. Cook the steak for 5 to 7 minutes per side, or until it reaches your desired level of doneness. Let the steak rest for a few minutes, then slice it thinly against the grain.

5. **Warm the tortillas.** Warm the tortillas in a dry skillet over medium heat, or in the microwave, until pliable.

6. **Assemble the burritos.** Lay each tortilla flat on a clean workspace. In the center of each tortilla, evenly distribute the flank steak and french fries and layer with shredded cheese, Greek yogurt, salsa, and avocado.

7. **Wrap the burritos.** Fold the sides of the tortilla over the filling, then roll it up tightly from the bottom. If desired, lightly toast the wrapped burritos in a dry skillet for a couple of minutes on each side to crisp them up.

8. **Serve.** Slice each burrito in half, and serve immediately, offering a satisfying and healthier twist on a classic favorite.

KOREAN BEEF WRAPS

The Korean Beef Wrap is one of my all-time favorites, blending bold Korean flavors with a healthy twist. The seasoned ground beef wrapped in a low-calorie tortilla brings back memories of my first job at a Korean fast-casual restaurant when I was 17. I fell in love with the vibrant and diverse flavors there, and this wrap is my way of enjoying those beloved tastes in a healthier, high-protein meal. It's a comforting reminder of my early days in the culinary world, and it always brings a smile to my face.

Yield: Makes 4
Prep time: 15 minutes
Cook time: 15 minutes
Total time: 30 minutes

FOR THE KOREAN BEEF

1lb lean ground beef
½ small onion, finely chopped
3 garlic cloves, minced
1 tbsp grated ginger
¼ cup low-sodium soy sauce
2 tbsp brown sugar or honey
1 tbsp rice vinegar
1 tbsp sesame oil
1 tsp red pepper flakes
  (optional)
Salt and pepper, to taste

FOR THE SAUCE

½ cup plain nonfat
  Greek yogurt
2 tbsp gochujang (Korean
  chili paste)
1 tbsp low-sodium soy sauce
1 tbsp rice vinegar
1 tsp honey or agave nectar
1 garlic clove, minced

TO SERVE

4–6 (8–10in) low-
  calorie tortillas
1 cup shredded lettuce
1 cup shredded carrots
1 cucumber, thinly sliced
Fresh cilantro leaves,
  to garnish (optional)
2 green onions, sliced,
  to garnish
1 tbsp sesame seeds,
  to garnish

1. **Prepare the Korean beef.** Heat a large skillet over medium-high heat. Add the ground beef, breaking it apart, and cook until browned. Drain any excess fat. Add the onion, garlic, and ginger. Cook for an additional 2 to 3 minutes, until the onion is softened.

2. **Season the beef.** Stir in the low-sodium soy sauce, brown sugar, rice vinegar, sesame oil, and red pepper flakes (if using). Cook for another 2 to 3 minutes, allowing the flavors to meld. Season with salt and pepper. Remove from the heat and set aside.

3. **Prepare the sauce.** In a small bowl, combine the Greek yogurt, gochujang, soy sauce, rice vinegar, honey, and garlic. Stir until smooth. Adjust the seasonings to taste.

4. **Warm the tortillas.** Heat the tortillas in a dry skillet over medium heat for about 30 seconds on each side, until warm and pliable.

5. **Assemble the wraps.** Place the tortillas on a clean workspace and spread a spoonful of the sauce down the center of each. Divide the Korean beef among the tortillas, then top with lettuce, carrots, cucumber, and cilantro leaves (if using). Garnish with green onions and sesame seeds.

6. **Serve.** Roll up the tortillas tightly around the filling, tucking in the sides as you go and serve immediately.

Bold flavors and textures wrapped in a soft tortilla!

GRILLED KOFTA PITA POCKETS WITH TAHINI-YOGURT SAUCE

The Grilled Kofta Pita Pockets with Tahini-Yogurt Sauce is a dish that takes me back to my Lebanese roots. When I was growing up, kofta was a staple in my family, and this recipe gives me all the nostalgia with fewer calories by mixing in lean ground beef. Despite being lighter, it's still incredibly juicy, and the tahini-yogurt sauce ties everything together beautifully. The low-calorie pitas are perfect for soaking up all those wonderful flavors. It's proof you can enjoy your cultural foods and stick to your nutrition goals at the same time!

Yield: Makes 4
Prep time: 15 minutes
Cook time: 10 minutes
Total time: 25 minutes

FOR THE KOFTA
½ lb ground lamb
½ lb lean ground beef
½ small onion, grated
2 garlic cloves, minced
2 tbsp chopped fresh
  parsley
1 tsp ground cumin
1 tsp ground coriander
½ tsp ground cinnamon
½ tsp paprika
¼ tsp cayenne pepper
  (optional)
Salt and pepper, to taste

FOR THE SAUCE
1 cup plain nonfat Greek
  yogurt
1 tbsp lemon juice
2 tbsp chopped fresh
  flat-leaf parsley or cilantro
½ tbsp chopped mint
2 garlic cloves, grated
2 tbsp tahini
Salt, to taste

TO SERVE
4 Joseph's Flax, Oat Bran &
  Whole Wheat pitas
1 cup shredded lettuce
1 cup halved cherry
  tomatoes
½ small red onion, thinly
  sliced
½ cucumber, sliced thinly
  into rounds or half-moons
¼ cup crumbled feta
  cheese (optional)

1. **Prepare the kofta.** In a large bowl, combine the ground lamb, ground beef, onion, garlic, parsley, cumin, coriander, cinnamon, paprika, cayenne pepper (if using), salt, and pepper. Mix well until combined. Shape into small, elongated patties or logs around 4 ounces each to make 4 patties.

2. **Cook the kofta.** Preheat a grill or skillet over medium-high heat. Cook the kofta patties for 3 to 4 minutes per side, or until browned on the outside and fully cooked through.

3. **Prepare the sauce.** In a small bowl, combine the Greek yogurt, lemon juice, parsley, mint, garlic, tahini, salt, and 2 to 3 tablespoons of water. Mix until smooth. Adjust the consistency with more water if needed.

4. **Assemble the pitas.** Warm the pita breads in a skillet or microwave. Cut each pita in half to form pockets. Fill each pita pocket with lettuce, cherry tomatoes, red onion, cucumber, and lamb kofta. Drizzle with the yogurt-tahini sauce and sprinkle with crumbled feta cheese (if using).

5. **Serve.** Serve the pita pockets immediately.

Note: If Joseph's low-calorie pitas are unavailable, use regular pita bread with pockets. If using pitas without pockets, layer the ingredients on top and fold like a taco as an alternative.

TURKEY PESTO WRAP

The Turkey Pesto Wrap is one of my go-to meals because it's so easy to make and full of flavor. I love how it's packed with healthy, high-protein ingredients like deli turkey breast and low-fat mozzarella cheese. Plus, the fresh flavors of baby spinach and roasted red peppers really make it delicious. This wrap is perfect for a quick, nutritious meal on the go.

Yield: Makes 4
Prep time: 10 minutes
Cook time: 5 minutes
Total time: 15 minutes

4 (10in) whole wheat or
  low-carb tortillas
¼ cup pesto sauce
16oz package deli turkey
  breast
1 cup baby spinach
½ cup sliced roasted red
  peppers
¼ cup shredded low-fat
  mozzarella cheese
1 avocado, sliced (optional)

1. **Spread the pesto.** Lay out the tortillas on a clean workspace and evenly spread 1 tablespoon of pesto sauce on each tortilla.
2. **Layer the ingredients.** On each tortilla, add 4 ounces of the deli turkey breast, then layer the baby spinach, roasted red peppers, shredded mozzarella cheese, and avocado slices (if using).
3. **Roll the wrap.** Carefully roll up each tortilla, tucking in the sides as you go to secure the ingredients.
4. **Toast the wraps.** Heat a nonstick skillet over medium heat. Place the wraps in the skillet seam-side down. Toast for 2 to 3 minutes per side, pressing gently with a spatula, until the cheese is melted and the tortillas are golden brown and crispy.
5. **Serve.** Cut each wrap in half and serve immediately.

PIZZA
PIZZA
PIZZA
PIZZA
PIZZA
PIZZA
PIZZA

KETO PIZZA DOUGH

This Keto Pizza Dough totally blew me away! You won't taste the egg, and it comes out light, fluffy, and crispy, so you'd never guess it's low calorie. Even my dad, who's usually a tough food critic, gave it a thumbs up. It's perfect for whipping up your favorite pizzas, like turkey pepperoni with shredded mozzarella and tomato sauce. Trust me, you won't believe how good this is!

Yield: Makes 1 personal pizza
Prep time: 10 minutes
Cook time: 15 minutes
Total time: 25 minutes

2 large egg whites
1 tbsp arrowroot starch
½ tsp garlic powder
½ tsp onion powder
½ tsp salt
½ tsp dried oregano

OPTIONAL TOPPINGS
Pepperoni
Artichokes
Sausage
Onion

1. **Preheat the oven** to 375°F. Line a baking sheet with parchment paper.
2. **Make the dough.** In a small bowl, whisk the egg whites to stiff peaks. (For efficiency, use a hand mixer instead of hand whipping.) Gently fold in the arrowroot starch, garlic powder, onion powder, salt, and dried oregano until well combined.
3. **Shape the dough.** Spread the mixture onto the lined baking sheet and shape it into a circle about 8 to 10 inches in diameter. Use an offset spatula to spread the dough evenly on the baking sheet for a consistent crust.
4. **Bake the crust.** Bake the dough for 8 to 10 minutes, or until the edges are golden and the crust is firm. For a firmer crust, bake an additional 2 to 3 minutes or until the edges are slightly crisp.
5. **Add the toppings.** Remove the crust from the oven, add cheese and your favorite keto-friendly toppings, and return to the oven for an additional 5 minutes, until the cheese is melted and bubbly.

Note: If arrowroot starch is unavailable, substitute with cornstarch for a similar result.

HEALTHIER PIZZA TOASTIES

Pizza toasties were a childhood favorite of mine—quick, cheesy, and oh-so-satisfying. This healthier version keeps all the flavor but uses lighter ingredients. With whole-grain bread, low-fat mozzarella, and your favorite toppings, these pizza toasties are the perfect snack or easy meal that won't derail your nutrition goals.

Yield: Makes 2
Prep time: 5 minutes
Cook time: 10 minutes
Total time: 15 minutes

2 slices whole-grain bread
2 tbsp marinara or pizza sauce
1/3 cup shredded low-fat
   mozzarella cheese
Toppings (your favorite healthy
   ones, such as turkey
   pepperoni, veggies, etc.)
Dried oregano, to taste

1. **Preheat the oven** to 375°F.
2. **Assemble the toasties.** Lay the bread slices flat on a plate or clean workspace. Spread the marinara on each slice. Sprinkle with the shredded mozzarella and add your favorite healthy toppings. Finish with a sprinkle of dried oregano.
3. **Bake the toasties.** Transfer the toasties to a baking sheet. Bake for 8 to 10 minutes, or until the cheese is melted and bubbly.
4. **Serve.** Slice and enjoy!

Cheesy, gooey goodness made lighter!

EASY HEALTHIER CHEESE PIZZA

Sometimes, you just need a quick-and-easy pizza fix, and this Easy Healthier Cheese Pizza using Joseph's Pita Bread hits the spot. It's super simple, lower in calories, and tastes delicious. Plus, it's a fun activity to do with the kids—they'll love helping out, and it's a great way to build their confidence in the kitchen!

Yield: Makes 1 personal pizza
Prep time: 5 minutes
Cook time: 10 minutes
Total time: 15 minutes

1 Joseph's Pita Bread
¼ cup marinara or pizza sauce (choose a lower sodium or lower sugar option, if desired)
⅓ cup shredded low-fat mozzarella cheese
½ tsp dried oregano
Pinch of red pepper flakes (optional)
Garlic powder (optional)

1. **Preheat the oven** to 400°F.
2. **Assemble the pizza.** Place the pita bread on a baking sheet. Spread the sauce evenly over the pita, leaving a small border around the edges. Sprinkle the shredded mozzarella over top and add the dried oregano and any other optional seasonings you like.
3. **Bake the pizza.** Bake for 8 to 10 minutes, or until the cheese is melted and bubbly and the edges of the pita are crisp.
4. **Serve.** Slice and enjoy!

Note: If Joseph's Pita Bread is not available, whole wheat or thin crust alternatives can also work well while maintaining a healthier profile. Nutritional values may vary based on the brand.

BARBECUE CHICKEN PIZZA WITH LAVASH BREAD

When I was growing up, my mom would take my sister and me to California Pizza Kitchen (CPK), where we'd have the greatest barbecue-chicken pizza ever. This recipe is an homage to that iconic dish. It's quick, delicious, and satisfies those CPK cravings without the extra calories.

Yield: Makes 1 personal pizza
Prep time: 10 minutes
Cook time: 9 minutes
Total time: 19 minutes

1 sheet of lavash bread

¼ cup barbecue sauce
(sugar-free, if preferred)

½ cup cooked and shredded
chicken breast

⅓ cup shredded low-fat
mozzarella cheese

¼ small red onion, thinly sliced

1 tbsp chopped fresh cilantro
(optional)

1. **Preheat the oven** to 400°F.
2. **Assemble the pizza.** Place the lavash bread on a baking sheet. Spread the barbecue sauce evenly over the lavash. Top with the shredded chicken, shredded mozzarella, and red onion. (Sprinkling a little of the cheese over the chicken and onions will help hold them in place.)
3. **Bake the pizza.** Bake for 6 to 9 minutes, or until the cheese is melted and bubbly and the edges of the lavash are golden brown. Monitor closely to avoid overcooking.
4. **Serve.** Sprinkle with the chopped cilantro (if using), slice, and enjoy!

Note: If lavash bread is unavailable, substitute with thin pita bread, naan, or a tortilla for similar results.

Sweet, smoky, and absolutely delicious.

COPYCAT DEL TACO CHICKEN SOFT TACOS

The first time I had a Del Taco chicken taco was in high school with my friends after football practice, and I legit ate ten of them because they were so good. This copycat recipe brings all that deliciousness home with a healthy twist. It's got that juicy, flavorful chicken and the perfect mix of toppings, all wrapped up in a warm, low-carb tortilla. Easy, tasty, and way better than takeout!

Yield: Makes 4
Prep time: 0 minutes
Cook time: 10 minutes
Total time: 10 minutes

1 tbsp olive oil
1lb boneless, skinless chicken
    breasts, diced
1 packet taco seasoning
4 small low-carb flour tortillas
½ cup shredded lettuce
½ cup diced tomatoes
¼ cup shredded cheddar cheese
¼ cup light sour cream
Hot sauce (optional)
Salsa (optional)

1. **Cook the chicken.** Heat a medium skillet over medium heat, then add the olive oil. Once the oil is hot, add the chicken and cook until it's no longer pink. Sprinkle in the taco seasoning and stir until the chicken is well coated. Cook for an additional 2 to 3 minutes until the chicken is fully cooked and evenly seasoned.

2. **Warm the tortillas.** While the chicken is cooking, warm the low-carb tortillas in a dry skillet over medium heat, or in the microwave, until soft and pliable.

3. **Assemble the tacos.** Place the tortillas on individual plates or a clean workspace. Divide the cooked chicken evenly among the tortillas. Top with lettuce, tomatoes, shredded cheese, and a dollop of sour cream. Add your favorite hot sauce or salsa (if using).

4. **Serve.** Fold the tacos in half and enjoy!

CRISPY BUFFALO-CHICKEN TACOS

Buffalo-chicken lovers, this one's for you! These Crispy Buffalo-Chicken Tacos are made in the air fryer or oven and combine that spicy, tangy flavor with a satisfying crunch. Wrapped in a warm tortilla and topped with all your favorite fixings, they're the perfect blend of heat and comfort—plus, they're healthier and super easy to make.

Yield: Makes 4
Prep time: 15 minutes
Cook time: 12–15 minutes (Air Fryer) or 20–25 minutes (Oven)
Total time: 27–40 minutes

1lb boneless, skinless chicken breasts, cut into strips
2 tbsp light mayo
1 tsp garlic powder
1 tsp onion powder
Salt and pepper, to taste
½ cup cornflakes breadcrumbs
Avocado oil spray
½ cup hot sauce (like Frank's RedHot)
4 small low-carb tortillas (either corn or flour)
½ cup shredded lettuce
¼ cup diced tomatoes
¼ cup light ranch or blue cheese dressing
Crumbled blue cheese (optional)
Avocado slices (optional)

1. **Preheat the air fryer** to 375°F, or the oven to 400°F.
2. **Prepare the chicken.** In a medium bowl, toss the chicken strips with the light mayo, garlic powder, onion powder, salt, and pepper until everything is well coated.
3. **Dredge the chicken.** To a small shallow bowl, add the cornflakes breadcrumbs. Dredge the mayo-coated chicken strips in the cornflakes breadcrumbs, pressing firmly to adhere. Spray the chicken strips with avocado oil on all sides.
4. **Cook the chicken.**
   Air fry: In an air-fryer basket, arrange the breaded chicken strips in a single layer. Cook for 12 to 15 minutes, flipping halfway through, until golden brown, crispy, and cooked through to 165°F.
   Oven: On a wire rack set over a baking sheet, place the breaded chicken strips. Bake for 20 to 25 minutes, flipping halfway through, until golden brown, crispy, and cooked through to 165°F.
5. **Warm the tortillas.** While the chicken is cooking, warm the tortillas in a dry skillet over medium heat, or in the microwave, until soft and pliable.
6. **Toss the crispy chicken in Buffalo sauce.** To a large bowl, add the hot sauce. Once the chicken strips are cooked and crispy, transfer them to the bowl with hot sauce and toss until evenly coated.
7. **Assemble the tacos.** Place the warmed tortillas on a plate. Divide the Buffalo chicken strips evenly among the tortillas. Top with the lettuce, tomatoes, and a drizzle of ranch or blue cheese dressing. Add the crumbled blue cheese and avocado (if using).
8. **Serve.** Fold the tacos in half and enjoy with all the spicy, tangy goodness you love!

CRISPY, BAKED BEEF TACOS

Back in high school, after football practice, I would have my mom take me to Jack in the Box to grab those greasy, crunchy tacos for just a dollar—and they gave you two! And let me tell you, they *always* hit different. Believe it or not, those cheap tacos were fire! This is my healthier version that hits all the right notes, satisfying those cravings with a little more balance.

Yield: Makes 6
Prep time: 10 minutes
Cook time: 10–12 minutes
Total time: 20–22 minutes

½lb lean ground beef
½ packet taco seasoning
6 corn tortillas
Avocado oil or avocado oil spray
½ cup shredded low-fat
  cheddar cheese
Optional toppings: lettuce,
  tomatoes, salsa, Greek yogurt
  (as a sour cream substitute)

1. **Preheat the oven** to 400°F. Line a baking sheet with parchment paper or foil.
2. **Cook the beef.** In a medium skillet over medium heat, cook the ground beef until browned. Add the ½ packet of taco seasoning, and stir until the beef is fully coated. Cook for an additional 2 to 3 minutes until the beef is fully cooked and evenly seasoned. Drain any excess fat to prevent the tacos from becoming greasy.
3. **Prepare the tortillas.** Microwave the tortillas with a damp towel for 20 to 30 seconds to make them easier to handle. Lightly brush or spray one side of each tortilla with avocado oil and place them on the lined baking sheet with the oiled side down.
4. **Assemble the tacos.** Divide the beef evenly among the corn tortillas. Sprinkle the shredded cheese over top and fold the tortillas in half.
5. **Bake the tacos.** Bake for 10 to 12 minutes, or until the tortillas are crispy and the cheese is melted.
6. **Serve.** Add your favorite toppings—like lettuce, tomatoes, salsa, and a dollop of Greek yogurt and enjoy!

Note: For extra crispy tacos, place another baking sheet on top of the tacos and weigh it down with a heavy pan, such as a cast-iron skillet, during the first half of baking time.

BIG MAC SMASH TACOS

Why settle for just one Big Mac when you can have five of these healthier Big Mac Smash Tacos? With low-carb tortillas, you get all the iconic Big Mac flavors in a lighter, more satisfying version. Plus, the homemade Big Mac Sauce is spot-on!

Yield: Makes 5
Prep time: 15 minutes
Cook time: 10 minutes
Total time: 25 minutes

FOR THE BIG MAC SAUCE

¾ cup plain nonfat Greek yogurt
¾ cup light mayo
3 tbsp sweet pickle relish
1 tbsp grated white onion
1 tbsp yellow mustard
1 tsp honey
½ tsp garlic powder
½ tsp onion powder
½ tsp paprika
½ tsp fine sea salt

FOR THE TACOS

1lb lean ground beef
½ tsp garlic powder
½ tsp onion powder
Salt and pepper, to taste
5 small low-carb tortillas
    (either corn or flour)
½ cup shredded iceberg lettuce
¼ cup diced onions
¼ cup chopped pickles
½ cup shredded low-fat cheddar cheese

1. **Prepare the sauce.** In a small bowl, mix together the Greek yogurt and mayo as the base. Add the relish, onion, mustard, honey, garlic powder, onion powder, paprika, and salt. Stir until well combined and set aside.

2. **Cook the beef.** Heat a large nonstick skillet over medium heat. Lightly spray the skillet with cooking spray to prevent sticking and add the ground beef, breaking it up as you go. Season with the garlic powder, onion powder, salt, and pepper. Cook until the beef is browned, about 5 minutes. Remove from the heat and drain any excess fat.

3. **Assemble the tacos.** Heat the tortillas in a dry skillet over medium heat, or the microwave, until soft and pliable. Place the tortillas on a clean workspace. Divide the cooked beef among the tortillas and smash slightly. Top with the lettuce, onions, pickles, and shredded cheese.

4. **Add the sauce.** Drizzle the Big Mac sauce over top to bring all the flavors together.

5. **Serve.** Fold the tortillas in half, and enjoy!

Note: For a true smash taco, press the beef directly onto the tortilla and smash it down into the pan to create a crispy, flavorful crust. Cook for 3 to 4 minutes per side on medium-high heat. After flipping, top the crispy cooked meat with one slice of Velveeta cheese and cook for 1 to 2 more minutes until the cheese begins to melt. Remove from the heat and top with shredded iceberg lettuce, onions, pickles, and 1 to 2 teaspoons of the Big Mac sauce.

The best of both worlds— burger meets taco!

Smoky, spicy,
seafood
perfection!

CHIPOTLE-SHRIMP TACOS WITH CREAMY SLAW

These Chipotle-Shrimp Tacos are packed with flavor and have just the right amount of spice. The creamy coleslaw adds a refreshing crunch, making these tacos a delicious and balanced meal.

Yield: Makes 6
Prep time: 25 minutes
Cook time: 5 minutes
Total time: 30 minutes

FOR THE SHRIMP

1lb large shrimp, peeled and deveined
2 tbsp chipotle peppers in adobo
   sauce, chopped
1 tbsp olive oil
1 tsp garlic powder
1 tsp onion powder
Salt and pepper, to taste

FOR THE CREAMY COLESLAW

¼ cup plain nonfat Greek yogurt
2 tbsp light mayo
1 tbsp apple-cider vinegar
1 tsp honey or maple syrup
¼ cup chopped fresh cilantro
¼ cup diced red onion
Salt and pepper, to taste
2 cups shredded cabbage (or coleslaw mix)

FOR THE TACOS

4 small corn tortillas
Lime wedges, to serve (optional)

1. **Marinate the shrimp.** In a medium bowl, toss the shrimp, chipotle peppers, olive oil, garlic powder, onion powder, salt, and pepper. Let marinate for at least 10 minutes.

2. **Prepare the creamy coleslaw.** While the shrimp marinates, in a large bowl, mix together the Greek yogurt, mayo, apple-cider vinegar, honey, cilantro, red onion, salt, and pepper. Toss with the cabbage until well coated.

3. **Cook the shrimp.** Heat a large nonstick skillet over medium-high heat. Add the shrimp and cook for 2 to 3 minutes per side, until they are opaque and cooked through.

4. **Warm the tortillas.** While the shrimp is cooking, warm the corn tortillas in a dry skillet over medium heat, or in the microwave, until they are soft and pliable.

5. **Assemble the tacos.** Place the tortillas on a clean workspace. Evenly divide the cooked shrimp among the tortillas. Top with the creamy coleslaw and fold each taco in half.

6. **Serve.** Serve with lime wedges on the side (if using) and enjoy!

Note: The number of tacos may vary depending on the size of the shrimp and tortillas used.

HEALTHIER BAJA FISH TACOS

These Healthier Baja Fish Tacos have that perfect crunch you're craving, with seasoned, crispy fish and fresh, vibrant toppings. Add a dollop of light sour cream, and you've got yourself an irresistible taco-night favorite.

Yield: Makes 4
Prep time: 20 minutes
Cook time: 8–10 minutes (Air Fryer) or 15–18 minutes (Oven)
Total time: 28–38 minutes

FOR THE FISH
½ cup panko breadcrumbs
¼ cup cornmeal
1 tsp chili powder
1 tsp cumin
½ tsp garlic powder
½ tsp onion powder
Salt and pepper, to taste
1 egg, beaten
1lb white fish fillets (like cod or tilapia)
Avocado oil spray

FOR THE TACOS
4 small corn tortillas
1 cup shredded cabbage
¼ cup diced tomatoes
¼ cup chopped fresh cilantro
¼ cup diced red onion
¼ cup light sour cream
Juice of 1 lime
Lime wedges, to serve
Sliced avocado, to serve (optional)
Salsa, to serve (optional)

1. **Preheat the air fryer** to 350°F, or the oven to 385°F.
2. **Prepare the fish coating.** In a shallow bowl, mix together the panko breadcrumbs, cornmeal, chili powder, cumin, garlic powder, onion powder, salt, and pepper.
3. **Bread the fish.** To a small shallow bowl, add the beaten egg. Dip each fish fillet into the beaten egg, then coat with the breadcrumb mixture, pressing firmly to adhere. Spray both sides of the coated fish with avocado oil.
4. **Cook the fish.**
   Air fryer: In an air-fryer basket, place the breaded fish fillets in a single layer. Cook for 8 to 10 minutes, flipping halfway through, until golden brown and crispy.
   Oven: On a baking sheet lined with parchment paper, place the breaded fish fillets. Bake for 15 to 18 minutes, flipping halfway through, until golden brown and crispy.
5. **Warm the tortillas.** While the fish is cooking, warm the corn tortillas in a dry skillet over medium heat, or in the microwave, until they are soft and pliable.
6. **Assemble the tacos.** Place the tortillas on a clean workspace. Divide the crispy fish evenly among the tortillas. Top with the shredded cabbage, diced tomatoes, cilantro, red onion, and light sour cream. Add a squeeze of lime juice for extra zest.
7. **Serve.** Serve with additional lime wedges and avocado (if using). Top with salsa (if using), and enjoy!

Note: For added texture and flavor, top the tacos with a creamy slaw. Mix ½ cup shredded cabbage, 1 tablespoon light mayo, 1 tablespoon plain nonfat Greek yogurt, 1 teaspoon lime juice, a pinch of salt and freshly cracked black pepper, 1 teaspoon rice vinegar, 1 teaspoon honey, and 1 tablespoon chopped fresh cilantro, for a quick and light slaw.

Crispy fish with a zesty kick and beach vibes in every bite.

BURGERS

BURGERS

BURGERS

BURGERS

BURGERS

BURGERS

BURGERS

TURKEY BURGER WITH LEMON AIOLI

When I was 19, I worked at a restaurant named G Burger, where I first fell in love with a turkey burger. This recipe is comparable in flavor and juiciness, and it brings back those memories every time. Grilling is my preferred method for cooking these burgers because it adds a nice smoky flavor, but you can also cook them on the stovetop for equally delicious results.

Yield: Makes 4
Prep time: 15 minutes
Cook time: 10 minutes
Total time: 25 minutes

FOR THE LEMON AIOLI

¼ cup light mayo
¼ cup plain nonfat Greek yogurt
Zest of 1 lemon
1 tbsp lemon juice
1 garlic clove, minced
Salt and pepper, to taste

FOR THE TURKEY BURGERS

1lb (93% lean) ground turkey
¾ tsp cornstarch or arrowroot starch
1 tsp garlic powder
1 tsp onion powder
½ tsp paprika
Salt and pepper, to taste
4 whole-wheat or low-carb buns

FOR THE TOPPINGS

1 cup mixed greens or lettuce
1 tomato, sliced
¼ red onion, thinly sliced

1. **Prepare the lemon aioli.** In a small bowl, mix together the mayo, Greek yogurt, lemon zest, lemon juice, minced garlic, salt, and pepper. Stir until well combined and set aside.
2. **Prepare the turkey patties.** In a large bowl, combine the ground turkey, cornstarch, garlic powder, onion powder, paprika, salt, pepper, and 1 tablespoon of water. Mix gently to combine, being careful not to overwork the meat. Divide into 4 equal portions and shape into patties.
3. **Cook the patties.**
   Grill: Preheat the grill to medium-high heat. Cook the patties for 4 to 5 minutes per side, or until they are cooked through and reach an internal temperature of 165°F.
   Stovetop: Heat a large skillet over medium-high heat. Cook the patties for 4 to 5 minutes per side, or until they are cooked through and reach an internal temperature of 165°F.
4. **Toast the buns.** While the patties are cooking, lightly toast the buns on the grill or in a toaster.
5. **Assemble the burgers.** Spread a generous amount of lemon aioli on each bun. Place each turkey patty on a bun and top with mixed greens, a slice of tomato, red onions, and any other desired toppings, like avocados or pickles. Finish with the top bun.
6. **Serve.** Enjoy your flavorful burger—light, zesty, and delicious!

COPYCAT SPICY MCCHICKEN SANDWICH

One of the first fast foods I ever fell in love with as a kid was the McChicken from McDonald's. My parents would grab one for me after a long playdate, and I was absolutely hooked. It even contributed to my chubby phase! Now, with this version, I get to relive those childhood memories but in a way that helps me stay on track with my nutrition goals. It's got all the flavors I loved but is way better for my health.

Yield: Makes 4

Prep time: 35 minutes

Cook time: 12–15 minutes (Air Fryer) or 20–25 minutes (Oven)

Total time: 47–60 minutes

FOR THE CHICKEN PATTIES

½ tsp garlic powder

½ tsp onion powder

½ tsp paprika

¾ tsp salt

½ tsp black pepper

¼ tsp cayenne pepper (optional)

1lb ground chicken

1 tsp cornstarch

½ cup cornflakes breadcrumbs

Avocado oil spray

FOR THE SANDWICH

4 brioche buns

4 tbsp light mayo

½ cup shredded lettuce

1. **Preheat the air fryer** to 375°F, or the oven to 400°F.
2. **Prepare the seasonings.** In a small bowl, mix together the garlic powder, onion powder, paprika, salt, pepper, and cayenne pepper (if using).
3. **Prepare the chicken patties.** In a large bowl, combine the ground chicken, cornstarch, and the seasoning mixture. Mix well and form into 4 equal-size patties. Place in the fridge for 15 to 20 minutes to firm up.
4. **Dredge the patties.** To a small bowl, add the cornflakes breadcrumbs. Coat each patty in the cornflakes, pressing firmly to adhere. Lightly spray the patties with avocado oil.
5. **Cook the patties.**
   Air fryer: To an air-fryer basket, place the breaded patties. Air-fry for 12 to 15 minutes, flipping halfway through, until golden and cooked through to an internal temperature of 165°F.
   Oven: On a wire rack set over a baking sheet, place the patties. Bake for 20 to 25 minutes, flipping halfway through, until golden and cooked through to an internal temperature of 165°F.
6. **Assemble the sandwiches.** Lightly toast the buns or microwave with a damp towel for 20 to 30 seconds, then spread a layer of light mayo on each. On each bun, place a crispy chicken patty, top with shredded lettuce, and finish with the top bun.
7. **Serve.** Enjoy your sandwich, full of flavor and spice without the extra fuss!

BURGERS **EXQUISITE EATS**

COPYCAT MCDONALD'S CHEESEBURGER

The McDonald's cheeseburger was my introduction to fast food. Whenever my parents wanted to treat us, that was what my dad would order for the whole family, along with fries. I remember him getting seven to eight cheeseburgers, and he'd end up eating most of them because he's a big guy at six foot three and has a solid appetite. The McDonald's cheeseburger still reminds me of my childhood, and I'll always love it. My version is higher in protein, using lean ground beef and Velveeta slices, which are only 40 calories per slice, so you don't have to give up the foods you love to reach your health goals.

Yield: Makes 5
Prep time: 10 minutes
Cook time: 10 minutes
Total time: 20 minutes

FOR THE BEEF PATTIES
½ tsp garlic powder
½ tsp onion powder
¾ tsp salt
½ tsp black pepper
1lb (93% lean) ground beef

FOR THE CHEESEBURGERS
5 Velveeta slices
5 brioche buns
¼ cup finely diced onions
10 slices of pickle
5 tsp ketchup
5 tsp mustard

1. **Prepare the seasonings.** In a small bowl, mix together the garlic powder, onion powder, salt, and pepper.
2. **Prepare the beef patties.** In a large bowl, add the ground beef and pour in the seasoning mixture. Mix the meat gently to combine, then form into 5 patties, each approximately 4 inches in diameter, ¼ inch thick, and weighing about 2 ounces to replicate the size of a McDonald's burger.
3. **Cook the patties.**
   Grill: Preheat the grill to medium-high heat. Cook the patties for 3 to 4 minutes per side until they reach your desired level of doneness.
   Stovetop: Heat a skillet over medium-high heat. Cook the patties for 3 to 4 minutes per side until they reach your desired level of doneness.
4. **Melt the cheese.** One minute before the patties are done, place a slice of Velveeta on each patty and allow to melt.
5. **Assemble the cheeseburgers.** Lightly toast the buns or microwave with a damp towel for 20 to 30 seconds. Place each patty on a brioche bun, top with the onions, pickles, ketchup, and mustard, and finish with the top bun.
6. **Serve.** Enjoy your homemade cheeseburger with all the nostalgic flavors, but healthier and more satisfying!

Note: For best results, before cooking the patties, press the center of each patty slightly with your thumb to prevent puffing.

Copycat McDonald's Cheeseburger

Copycat McDonald's Big Mac

Two all-beef patties, special sauce, lettuce, cheese, pickles, onions, on a sesame seed bun! IYKYK

COPYCAT MCDONALD'S BIG MAC

Growing up in Saudi Arabia, my friends and I would gather around the pool on the weekends, chowing down on McDonald's. The Big Mac quickly became my favorite—I always ordered it, and it just hit differently. This version of the Big Mac keeps all those flavors I loved but is lower in calories. The sauce ties everything together, making it taste just like the original but with a healthy twist.

Yield: Makes 4
Prep time: 15 minutes
Cook time: 10 minutes
Total time: 25 minutes

FOR THE BEEF PATTIES

½ tsp garlic powder
½ tsp onion powder
¾ tsp salt
½ tsp black pepper
1lb (93% lean) ground beef

FOR THE BIG MACS

1 batch **Big Mac Sauce** (pg. 90)
8 Velveeta slices
6 keto or brioche buns
  (4 bottoms, 4 middles,
  4 tops)
16 hamburger dill pickle chips,
  oval cut
½ cup finely diced white
  onions
1 cup shredded iceberg lettuce

1. **Prepare the seasonings.** In a small bowl, mix together the garlic powder, onion powder, salt, and pepper.
2. **Prepare the beef patties.** In a large bowl, add the ground beef and pour in the seasoning mixture. Mix gently to combine, then form into 8 patties, each about 4 inches in diameter, ¼ inch thick, and weighing about 2 ounces, to replicate the thin patties characteristic of a Big Mac.
3. **Cook the patties.**
   Grill: Preheat the grill to medium-high heat. Cook the patties for 2 to 3 minutes per side, or until they reach your desired level of doneness.
   Stovetop: Lightly spray a skillet with nonstick cooking spray and heat over medium-high heat. Cook the patties for 2 to 3 minutes per side, until they reach your desired level of doneness.
4. **Prepare the buns.** Slice four of the bun halves to create the middle buns. To enhance the flavor, lightly toast the buns for 1 to 2 minutes over medium heat, or microwave them with a damp towel for 20 to 30 seconds.
5. **Assemble the Big Macs.**
   Bottom bun: Spread 1 to 2 teaspoons of the sauce on the bottom bun, top with 1 teaspoon of onions, then 1 to 2 tablespoons of iceberg lettuce, then 1 slice of cheese, and top with 1 beef patty.
   Middle bun: Spread 1 to 2 teaspoons of sauce on the middle bun, add a layer of 1 teaspoon of onions, then 1 to 2 tablespoons of lettuce, then 2 to 3 pickles, and top with another beef patty.
   Assemble the Big Mac: Take the middle bun with all the fixings on it and place it on top of the loaded bottom bun, then finish it off with the top bun. (The top bun is dry, but you can add 1 teaspoon of the sauce to the top bun for a saucier experience!)
6. **Serve.** Enjoy your homemade Big Mac with all the nostalgic flavors, but with fewer calories!

Note: For the ultimate copycat Big Mac, I strongly suggest following step 5 ("Assemble the Big Macs") precisely, as it's how McDonald's does it! If keto buns are too dry, substitute with St. Pierre brioche buns or regular sesame seed buns for better texture.

COPYCAT WHOPPER

As kids, whenever we got tired of McDonald's, my friends and I would mix it up by ordering Burger King. The Whopper quickly became one of my all-time favorite fast-food burgers—seriously underrated. This version brings back all those childhood memories and flavors, but made right at home.

Yield: Makes 4
Prep time: 15 minutes
Cook time: 10 minutes
Total time: 25 minutes

FOR THE BEEF PATTIES

½ tsp garlic powder
½ tsp onion powder
¾ tsp salt
½ tsp black pepper
1lb (93% lean) ground beef

FOR THE WHOPPERS

4 sesame seed buns
4 tbsp light mayo
4 Velveeta slices
4 tbsp ketchup
16 pickle chips
¼ cup thinly sliced
   white onions
4 slices of tomato
1 cup shredded or
   chopped iceberg lettuce

1. **Prepare the seasonings.** In a small bowl, mix together the garlic powder, onion powder, salt, and pepper.
2. **Prepare the beef patties.** In a large bowl, combine the ground beef with the seasoning mixture. Mix gently to combine, then form into 4 patties, approximately 4 to 5 inches in diameter and ¼ inch thick to replicate the thin, wide patties characteristic of a Whopper.
3. **Cook the patties.**
   Grill: Preheat the grill to medium-high heat. Cook the patties for 3 to 4 minutes per side, or until they reach your desired level of doneness.
   Stovetop: Lightly spray a skillet with nonstick cooking spray and heat over medium-high heat. Cook the patties for 3 to 4 minutes per side, or until they reach your desired level of doneness.
4. **Assemble the Whoppers.** Layer the ingredients in the traditional Whopper order: On the bottom bun, spread 1 tablespoon of the mayo, add a cooked patty, and place a slice of cheese on top. To the top bun, add one-quarter each of the ketchup, pickles, onions, tomato, and lettuce. Flip the loaded top bun over the cheese-covered patty.
5. **Serve.** Enjoy your homemade Whopper, packed with all the nostalgic flavors and just as delicious as the original!

Note: I suggest using the grill method to cook the patties to get that smoky Whopper flavor!

Cheese-
stuffed
goodness!

HEALTHIER COPYCAT JUICY LUCY BURGER

Get ready for a burger experience that will blow your mind! This healthier take on the Juicy Lucy still packs in all that cheesy, juicy goodness. Using lean ground beef and stuffing it with melty Velveeta or American cheese, you get that iconic ooey-gooey center without the extra calories. And when you throw it all on a keto or brioche bun, you've got a burger that's not only satisfying but also a little bit better for you.

Yield: Makes 3
Prep time: 15 minutes
Cook time: 10 minutes
Total time: 25 minutes

1lb (93% lean) ground beef
Salt and pepper, to taste
½ tsp garlic powder
3 Velveeta slices or American cheese slices
3 keto or brioche buns
Optional toppings: lettuce, tomato, pickles, onions, ketchup, mustard

1. **Prepare the beef patties.** Divide the lean ground beef into 6 equal portions (about 2.7 ounces each). Flatten each portion into a thin patty, each 4 inches in diameter and ¼ inch thick. Season the patties with salt, pepper, and garlic powder.
2. **Add the cheese.** Place a slice of cheese each on the centers of 3 of the patties, folding the cheese to fit if necessary. Place the other 3 patties on top, carefully sealing the edges to enclose the cheese.
3. **Cook the patties.** Preheat a grill or skillet over medium-high heat. Cook the patties for 3 to 4 minutes per side, or until they are cooked to your desired doneness and the cheese inside is melted. Avoid pressing down on the patties to prevent the cheese from leaking out. Once cooked, let the patties rest on a plate, loosely covered with foil, for 2 to 3 minutes. Resting allows the juices to redistribute, ensuring a juicier burger.
4. **Assemble the burgers.** Toast the keto or brioche buns on the grill or in a skillet, if desired. Place the cooked Juicy Lucy patties on the buns and add your favorite toppings, such as lettuce, tomato, pickles, onions, ketchup, and mustard.
5. **Serve.** Enjoy your burger with all the cheesy goodness you've been craving!

HEALTHIER COPYCAT IN-N-OUT DOUBLE-DOUBLE

The first time I tried In-N-Out was on my first day in the US. After winning the green-card lottery, my family and I arrived following a brutal 16-hour flight. We went to In-N-Out, where I took a bite of this burger and was blown away. It's the GOAT of burgers—you just can't live in California without loving it!

Yield: Makes 4
Prep time: 15 minutes
Cook time: 10 minutes
Total time: 25 minutes

FOR THE BEEF PATTIES

½ tsp garlic powder
½ tsp onion powder
¾ tsp salt
½ tsp black pepper
1lb (93% lean) ground beef

FOR THE SPECIAL SAUCE

¼ cup nonfat Greek yogurt
¼ cup light mayo
2 tbsp sweet pickle relish
1 tbsp ketchup
1 tsp yellow mustard
1 tsp white vinegar
½ tsp garlic powder
½ tsp onion powder
½ tsp paprika

FOR THE DOUBLE-DOUBLES

½ white onion, thinly sliced
8 Velveeta slices
4 brioche buns
8 tomato slices
8 lettuce leaves, folded in half

1. **Prepare the seasonings.** In a small bowl, mix together the garlic powder, onion powder, salt, and pepper.
2. **Prepare the beef patties.** In a large bowl, combine the ground beef with the seasoning mixture. Mix gently to combine, then form into 8 patties, each about 4 inches in diameter and ¼ inch thick to replicate the classic double-double size.
3. **Prepare the special sauce.** In a small bowl, mix together the Greek yogurt, mayo, relish, ketchup, mustard, white vinegar, garlic powder, onion powder, and paprika. Stir until well combined.
4. **Cook the patties.**
   Grill: Preheat the grill to medium-high heat. Cook the patties for 2 to 3 minutes per side, or until they reach your desired level of doneness. In the last minute of cooking, top with the cheese slices. Stack 2 patties, and set aside. Repeat for the remaining patties.
   If using onions, place the thinly sliced onion disc on top of the cheese patty, then top it with the other cheese patty so that the onion is sandwiched between them both.
   Stovetop: Spray a skillet with nonstick cooking spray and heat over high heat. Cook the patties for 2 to 3 minutes per side, or until they reach your desired level of doneness. In the last minute of cooking, top with the cheese slices. Stack 2 patties, and set aside. Repeat for the remaining patties.
   If using onions, place the thinly sliced onion disc on top of the cheese patty, then top it with the other cheese patty so that the onion is sandwiched between them both.
5. **Prepare the buns.** Lightly toast the buns or microwave them with a damp towel for 10 to 15 seconds, then assemble. If using keto buns, spread a thin layer of sauce to make them less dry.
6. **Assemble the Double-Doubles.** To the bottom bun, add a spoonful of special sauce, a slice of tomato, and two folded lettuce leaves. Place the double-patties stack over the lettuce and finish it off with the top bun. Repeat for the 3 remaining Double-Doubles.
7. **Serve.** Enjoy your healthier version of the In-N-Out Double-Double, packed with all the flavors you love, but lower in calories!

That's what a hamburger's ALL ABOUT!

HEALTHIER STEAKHOUSE BURGER

This Healthier Steakhouse Burger is packed with flavor and satisfies that craving for a hearty, juicy burger without all the extra calories. It's got all the elements you love from a steakhouse burger but made lighter with lean beef and a few healthy swaps.

Yield: Makes 4
Prep time: 15 minutes
Cook time: 10 minutes
Total time: 25 minutes

FOR THE BURGERS

1lb (93% lean) ground beef
1 tbsp Worcestershire sauce
1 tsp garlic powder
1 tsp onion powder
Salt and pepper, to taste
½ cup shredded light cheddar
   or Swiss cheese
4 whole wheat or low-carb buns

FOR THE TOPPINGS

1 cup mixed greens or lettuce
1 tomato, sliced
¼ red onion, thinly sliced
Optional: pickles, light mayo,
   mustard, ketchup

1. **Prepare the seasonings.** In a small bowl, combine the Worcestershire sauce, garlic powder, onion powder, salt, and pepper.

2. **Prepare the beef patties.** In a large bowl, combine the ground beef with the seasoning mixture. Mix gently to combine, being careful not to overwork the meat. Shape the patties to be 4 to 5 inches in diameter, ½ inch thick, and weighing about 6 ounces each.

3. **Cook the patties.** Heat a grill or skillet over medium-high heat. Cook the patties for 4 to 5 minutes per side, or until they reach your desired level of doneness. One minute before the patties are done, evenly distribute the cheese over each patty and allow to melt for the last minute of cooking. Once the patties are cooked, let them rest on a plate, loosely covered with foil, for 3 to 5 minutes. Resting allows the juices to redistribute, ensuring a juicier burger.

4. **Toast the buns.** While the patties rest, lightly toast the buns on the grill or in a toaster.

5. **Assemble the burgers.** Place each patty on a bun and top with mixed greens, tomato, red onions, and any other desired toppings, like pickles, mayo, mustard, or ketchup.

6. **Serve.** Enjoy your burger packed with flavor!

Note: Cook the burgers to your preferred doneness. For guidance, use an instant-read thermometer: 125°F for rare, 135°F for medium-rare, 145°F for medium, and 160°F for well-done.

HEALTHIER CHICKEN PARMESAN

Chicken parmesan is a classic Italian dish that I've always loved, but I wanted to make it more macro friendly without losing that authentic taste. This version keeps the crispy chicken, rich tomato sauce, and melty cheese, but pairs them with healthier ingredients, so you can enjoy all the flavors you love while staying on track with your health goals.

Yield: Serves 4
Prep time: 15 minutes
Cook time: 30 minutes
Total time: 45 minutes

FOR THE CHICKEN
4 (4oz) boneless, skinless
  chicken breasts
½ cup Italian breadcrumbs
¼ cup grated Parmesan cheese
½ tsp garlic powder
½ tsp onion powder
½ tsp dried oregano
¼ tsp salt
¼ tsp black pepper
½ cup all-purpose flour
2 large eggs, beaten
Olive oil spray

FOR THE SAUCE
1 garlic clove, minced
1 (14oz) can crushed tomatoes
  (no salt added)
½ tsp dried basil
½ tsp dried oregano
Salt and pepper, to taste

FOR THE TOPPINGS
½ cup shredded part-skim
  mozzarella cheese
¼ cup chopped fresh basil
  (optional, to garnish)

1. **Preheat the oven** to 400°F and line a baking sheet with parchment paper.
2. **Prepare the chicken.** Thinly slice the chicken breasts, or placing them between 2 sheets of plastic wrap or parchment paper, pound them to an even thickness of about ½ inch using a meat mallet or rolling pin.
3. **Dredge the chicken.** In a shallow dish, combine the breadcrumbs, Parmesan, garlic powder, onion powder, oregano, salt, and pepper. In 2 separate dishes, add the flour and beaten eggs. Coat each chicken breast in flour first, then dip in the beaten eggs, and lastly press into the breadcrumb mixture. Place the breaded chicken on the lined baking sheet. Lightly spray the chicken with olive oil spray.
4. **Bake the chicken.** Bake for 25 minutes on a wire rack set over a baking sheet, until the chicken is golden brown and cooked through to 165°F.
5. **Prepare the sauce.** While the chicken is baking, heat a small saucepan over medium heat. Spray with olive oil spray and sauté the garlic for 1 to 2 minutes, until fragrant. Add the crushed tomatoes, dried basil, oregano, salt, and pepper. Stir and let simmer for 10 minutes.
6. **Assemble and bake.** When the chicken is done cooking, remove from the oven. Spoon 2 to 3 spoonfuls of the tomato sauce over each piece and sprinkle with shredded mozzarella. Return the chicken to the oven and bake for an additional 5 minutes, or until the cheese is melted and bubbly.
7. **Serve.** Garnish with fresh basil (if using), and enjoy all the authentic flavors you love!

Healthier Chicken Parmesan

Healthier Copycat Panda Express Orange Chicken

HEALTHIER COPYCAT PANDA EXPRESS ORANGE CHICKEN

Back in the day, my mom would drive me to Panda Express between 6 p.m. and 7 p.m. on weekdays, sometimes even multiple times a week. At that age, I was always trying to get bigger and put on muscle since I played defensive end, and this dish was my go-to. The flavors were incredible—sweet, tangy, with just the right amount of savory goodness. This healthier version keeps those bold flavors and crispy textures but in a way that's more aligned with your health goals.

Yield: Serves 4
Prep time: 30 minutes
Cook time: 10–12 minutes (Air Fryer) or 15–18 minutes (Oven)
Total time: 40–48 minutes

FOR THE CHICKEN
1 egg white
1 tbsp soy sauce (or tamari, for a gluten-free substitute)
½ tsp white pepper
1 tbsp cornstarch
1½lbs boneless, skinless chicken thighs, cut into bite-size pieces

FOR THE DREDGE
½ cup all-purpose flour
¼ cup cornstarch
Avocado oil spray

FOR THE ORANGE SAUCE
½ cup freshly squeezed orange juice
¼ cup soy sauce or tamari
2 tbsp rice vinegar
4 tbsp honey
2 tbsp light brown sugar, packed
2 tsp orange zest
2 garlic cloves, minced
1 tsp minced ginger
¼ tsp red pepper flakes (optional, for spice)
2 tsp cornstarch

1. **Marinate the chicken.** In a large bowl, whisk together the egg white, soy sauce, white pepper, cornstarch, and 1 tablespoon of water. Add the chicken, toss to coat, and let marinate for at least 15 minutes.
2. **Preheat the air fryer** to 400°F, or the oven to 425°F.
3. **Dredge the chicken.** In a separate medium bowl, combine the flour and cornstarch. Dredge each piece of marinated chicken in the flour mixture, shaking off any excess.
4. **Cook the chicken.**
   Air fryer: Lightly spray the chicken with avocado oil. In the air-fryer basket, arrange the breaded chicken in a single layer. Cook for 10 to 12 minutes, flipping halfway through, until golden and crispy and cooked through to an internal temperature of 165°F.
   Oven: On a wire rack set over a baking sheet, place the breaded chicken. Spray lightly with avocado oil and bake for 15 to 18 minutes, flipping halfway through, until golden and crispy and cooked through to an internal temperature of 165°F.
5. **Make the orange sauce.** While the chicken is cooking, in a small saucepan over medium heat, combine the orange juice, soy sauce, rice vinegar, honey, brown sugar, orange zest, garlic, ginger, and red pepper flakes (if using). In a small bowl, whisk together the cornstarch and 1 tablespoon cold water to create a cornstarch slurry. Bring the orange sauce to a simmer, then add the cornstarch slurry. Cook for 2 to 3 minutes, stirring constantly, until the sauce thickens.
6. **Combine and serve.** Once the chicken is cooked, toss it in the orange sauce until evenly coated. Serve immediately with steamed rice and a side of veggies for a complete meal.

crispy, tangy, and just like takeout!

COPYCAT PANDA EXPRESS TERIYAKI CHICKEN

If you're looking for a high-protein, flavor-packed dish, this healthier Copycat Panda Express Teriyaki Chicken is it. Using chicken thighs keeps the meat juicy and tender, and the simple teriyaki glaze gives it that perfect balance of sweet and savory. This dish is incredibly easy to make, so you can enjoy a delicious, protein-rich meal without spending hours in the kitchen.

Yield: Serves 4
Prep time: 10 minutes
Cook time: 10–12 minutes (Air Fryer) or 15–18 minutes (Oven)
Total time: 20–28 minutes

FOR THE CHICKEN
1½lbs boneless, skinless chicken thighs
½ tsp salt
¼ tsp black pepper
½ tsp garlic powder
Avocado oil spray

FOR THE TERIYAKI SAUCE
⅓ cup low-sodium soy sauce
¼ cup honey
2 tbsp rice vinegar
1 tbsp light brown sugar, packed
1 garlic clove, minced
1 tsp minced fresh ginger
1 tbsp cornstarch
1 tbsp sesame seeds (optional, to garnish)
2 green onions, chopped (optional, to garnish)

1. **Preheat the air fryer** to 400°F, or the oven to 425°F.
2. **Prepare the chicken.** Season the chicken thighs with salt, pepper, and garlic powder. Lightly spray with avocado oil.
3. **Cook the chicken.**
   Air fryer: In an air-fryer basket, place the chicken thighs in a single layer. Cook for 10 to 12 minutes, flipping halfway through, until the chicken is cooked through to an internal temperature of 165°F and has a nice crispy exterior.
   Oven: On a baking sheet lined with parchment paper, place the chicken thighs. Bake for 15 to 18 minutes, flipping halfway through, until the chicken is crispy and cooked through to an internal temperature of 165°F.
4. **Make the teriyaki sauce.** While the chicken is cooking, in a small saucepan over medium heat, combine the soy sauce, honey, rice vinegar, brown sugar, garlic, ginger, and ¼ cup water. In a small bowl, whisk together the cornstarch and 2 tablespoons cold water to create a cornstarch slurry. Bring the sauce to a simmer, then add the cornstarch slurry to the saucepan. Cook for 5 to 6 minutes, stirring constantly, or until the sauce thickens enough to coat the back of a spoon.
5. **Combine and serve.** Once the chicken is cooked, slice it into strips and toss in the teriyaki sauce until evenly coated. Serve immediately with steamed rice and a side of veggies. Garnish with sesame seeds and green onions (if using).

ONE-PAN LEMON-CHICKEN ORZO PASTA

You know those days when you need something quick, easy, and delicious? This One-Pan Lemon-Chicken Orzo Pasta is perfect for those moments. The dish is creamy, zesty, and packed with flavor—all in just one pan, making cleanup a breeze. The Fairlife milk adds a creamy touch without being too heavy, and the lemon brightens everything up. Whether you're rushing after a long day or just want a satisfying meal with minimal effort, this dish has got you covered.

Yield: Serves 4
Prep time: 10 minutes
Cook time: 25 minutes
Total time: 35 minutes

FOR THE CHICKEN
1 tsp garlic powder
1 tsp onion powder
½ tsp paprika
½ tsp dried oregano
½ tsp salt
¼ tsp black pepper
½ tsp chili flakes (optional)
3 tbsp olive oil, divided
1lb chicken breasts, cut into
   bite-size pieces

FOR THE ORZO
3 garlic cloves, minced
1 cup uncooked orzo pasta
1 ½ cups chicken broth
½ cup Fairlife 2% milk
¼ cup grated Parmesan cheese
Juice and zest of 1 lemon
1 tbsp chopped fresh parsley
   (optional, to garnish)

1. **Season the chicken.** In a large bowl, mix together the garlic powder, onion powder, paprika, oregano, salt, pepper, and chili flakes (if using), then drizzle 2 tablespoons of olive oil and combine to make a paste. Toss the chicken in the seasoning paste and mix until well coated.

2. **Cook the chicken.** Preheat a large pan over medium-high heat for 4 minutes, then add the remaining 1 tablespoon of olive oil. Once the oil is hot, add the seasoned chicken and cook for 5 to 7 minutes, until the chicken is browned and cooked through to an internal temperature of 165°F. Remove from the pan and lightly tent with foil to let rest.

3. **Cook the orzo.** In the same pan, add the garlic, and sauté for 1 to 2 minutes, until fragrant. Add the uncooked orzo pasta and stir to coat. Pour in the chicken broth and bring to a simmer. Cook for 8 to 10 minutes, stirring occasionally, until the orzo is tender and most of the liquid is absorbed.

4. **Add the creaminess.** Once the orzo is tender, stir in the Fairlife milk, grated Parmesan, and lemon juice and zest. Return the cooked chicken to the pan, and stir to combine. Cook for another 2 to 3 minutes, until everything is heated through and creamy.

5. **Serve.** Garnish with fresh parsley (if using) and serve this creamy, zesty dish immediately. Enjoy the convenience of a one-pan meal that's bursting with flavor!

ONE-PAN KOREAN FRIED CHICKEN

When I was 17, I got my first job working at a Korean fast-casual restaurant—think Chipotle but with Korean food—and I quickly fell in love with the cuisine. To this day, it's one of my favorite cuisines ever. This dish is my high-protein homage to one of my favorite Korean dishes. It's got all the bold, spicy, and savory flavors that Korean food is known for, and I hope my version does it justice.

Yield: Serves 4
Prep time: 15 minutes
Cook time: 15 minutes
Total time: 30 minutes

FOR THE CHICKEN

½ cup cornstarch
¼ cup all-purpose flour
½ tsp salt
½ tsp black pepper
½ tsp garlic powder
1½lbs chicken breasts, cut into small 1-in cubes

FOR THE KOREAN SAUCE

3 tbsp gochujang (Korean chili paste)
2 tbsp soy sauce (or tamari, for a gluten-free substitute)
2 tbsp honey
1 tbsp rice vinegar
1 tbsp sesame oil
2 garlic cloves, minced
1 tsp minced ginger
1 tbsp brown sugar, packed
1 tsp sesame seeds (optional, to garnish)
2 green onions, chopped (optional, to garnish)

1. **Prepare the chicken.** In a large bowl, combine the cornstarch, flour, salt, pepper, and garlic powder. Dredge the cubed chicken in the mixture, making sure each piece is well coated.

2. **Cook the chicken.** Heat a large nonstick pan over medium-high heat. Lightly spray the pan with avocado oil. In a single layer, add the chicken cubes to the pan and cook for 8 to 10 minutes, flipping occasionally, until the chicken is golden brown and crispy on all sides and cooked through to an internal temperature of 165°F.

3. **Make the Korean sauce.** While the chicken is cooking, in a small bowl, mix together the gochujang, soy sauce, honey, rice vinegar, sesame oil, garlic, ginger, and brown sugar.

4. **Combine and glaze.** Once the chicken is cooked through, pour the Korean sauce over the chicken in the pan. Toss the chicken in the sauce and cook for another 2 to 3 minutes, allowing the sauce to thicken and coat the chicken evenly.

5. **Serve.** Garnish with sesame seeds and chopped green onions (if using). Enjoy this spicy, savory, and slightly sweet Korean fried chicken that's packed with flavor and protein!

HONEY-CHIPOTLE CHICKEN RICE BOWL

When I realized I didn't have to suffer through bland chicken and rice to stay on track, it was mind-blowing. This Honey-Chipotle Chicken Rice Bowl takes chicken and rice to the next level with a smoky, sweet, and tangy sauce that's perfectly balanced and satisfying. It's the kind of meal that makes healthy eating exciting and delicious.

Yields: Serves 4
Prep time: 15 minutes
Cook time: 35 minutes
Total time: 50 minutes

FOR THE RICE

1 cup uncooked brown or jasmine rice
2 cups low-sodium chicken broth or water
½ tsp salt

FOR THE CHICKEN

2 tbsp honey
2 tbsp chipotle-chili powder
1 tsp smoked paprika
1 tsp garlic powder
½ tsp onion powder
½ tsp ground cumin
½ tsp salt
¼ tsp black pepper
1½ lbs boneless, skinless chicken breasts, cut into bite-size pieces
1 tbsp olive oil

FOR THE SAUCE

2 garlic cloves, minced
¼ cup low-sodium chicken broth
2 tbsp honey
2 tbsp finely chopped chipotle in adobo sauce
1 tbsp light soy sauce
1 tsp cornstarch

FOR THE TOPPINGS

1 avocado, diced
½ cup corn kernels (canned, or frozen and thawed)
½ cup black beans, drained and rinsed
¼ cup chopped fresh cilantro
¼ cup queso fresco or low-fat feta cheese, crumbled
1 lime, cut into wedges

1. **Cook the rice.** In a medium saucepan over high heat, combine the rice, chicken broth, and salt. Bring to a boil, then reduce the heat to low, cover, and simmer for 15 to 20 minutes, or until the rice is cooked and fluffy. Set aside.

2. **Prepare the chicken.** In a large bowl, mix together the honey, chipotle-chili powder, smoked paprika, garlic powder, onion powder, cumin, salt, and pepper. Add the chicken, and toss to coat evenly.

3. **Cook the chicken.** In a large skillet over medium-high heat, add the olive oil. Once the oil is hot, add the seasoned chicken and cook for 6 to 8 minutes, stirring occasionally, until the chicken is caramelized and cooked through to 165°F.

4. **Make the sauce.** To the same skillet with the chicken, add the minced garlic and sauté for 1 to 2 minutes, until fragrant. In a separate bowl, whisk together the chicken broth, honey, chipotle in adobo sauce, soy sauce, and ¼ cup of water. Pour the sauce over the cooked chicken in the skillet. Bring to a simmer and cook for 2 to 3 minutes. Meanwhile, in a small bowl, combine the cornstarch with 2 teaspoons of cold water and mix together to create a cornstarch slurry. Add the cornstarch slurry to the skillet and continue to simmer for another 2 to 3 minutes, until the sauce thickens and coats the chicken.

5. **Assemble the bowls.** Divide the cooked rice among 4 bowls. Top each with the honey-chipotle chicken and spoon extra sauce over top. Add the diced avocado, corn, black beans, cilantro, and crumbled queso fresco.

6. **Serve.** Squeeze fresh lime juice over each bowl before serving for an added tangy finish.

HIGH-PROTEIN MAC 'N' CHEESE

When we were growing up, my mom would serve me and my sister mac 'n' cheese on Sunday afternoons. It's a dish that brings back fond memories of warmth and comfort. This protein-packed version uses chickpea or Barilla Protein+ pasta, cottage cheese, and Fairlife milk, giving you all the cheesy goodness with a nutritional boost. It's a reimagined version that keeps the nostalgia but supports your health goals.

Yield: Serves 4
Prep time: 10 minutes
Cook time: 15 minutes
Total time: 25 minutes

8oz chickpea or Barilla
 Protein+ elbows pasta
¾ cup low-fat cottage cheese
¾ cup Fairlife 2% milk
 (adjust as needed)
1 packet (about 1oz) mac 'n'
 cheese powder
3 Velveeta slices, torn into pieces
½ tsp garlic powder
½ tsp onion powder
½ tsp smoked paprika
¼ cup shredded low-fat cheddar
 cheese (optional, for extra
 cheesiness)
½ tsp salt
¼ tsp black pepper
Optional toppings: chopped
 parsley, paprika, additional
 cheese

1. **Cook the pasta.** Bring a large pot of water to a boil over high heat. Add the pasta and cook according to package instructions until al dente, about 8 to 10 minutes. Reserve ¼ cup of pasta water, then drain the pasta and set aside.

2. **Make the cheese sauce.** In a blender or food processor, combine the cottage cheese, Fairlife milk, and mac 'n' cheese powder and blend until smooth. To a medium pot over low heat, add the milk-and-cheese mixture. Next, add the torn Velveeta slices, garlic powder, onion powder, and smoked paprika. Stir constantly for 5 to 7 minutes, ensuring the sauce is smooth and heated through. Add the reserved pasta water 1 tablespoon at a time until you achieve a creamy consistency. Be careful not to overheat the mixture to prevent the cottage cheese from splitting.

3. **Combine.** Add the cooked pasta back into the pot with the cheese sauce and stir until the pasta is evenly coated. If using, stir in the shredded low-fat cheddar cheese for extra creaminess.

4. **Season and serve.** Season with the salt and black pepper. Garnish with optional toppings like chopped parsley, paprika, or extra cheese for added flavor (if using), and serve immediately.

5. **Enjoy.** Dig into this High-Protein Mac 'N' Cheese, which is sure to bring back those cozy childhood memories but in a way that aligns with your nutritional goals!

HONEY-BARBECUE SLOW-COOKER MEATBALLS

What are the qualities of a perfect recipe? 1) Easy to make, 2) minimal cleanup, and 3) *insane* flavor. This Honey-Barbecue Slow-Cooker Meatballs recipe is all that—and more. Imagine prepping everything in the morning before heading to work or taking the kids to school and coming home to a house filled with the mouthwatering aroma of sweet, tangy, smoky meatballs. The dish is effortless, cleanup is a breeze, and the flavor? Absolutely out of this world.

Yield: Serves 4–6
Prep time: 10 minutes
Cook time: 2–3 hours on high, or 4–6 hours on low
Total time: 2–6 hours

FOR THE MEATBALLS
1½lbs ground beef
  (or ground turkey)
½ cup breadcrumbs
¼ cup grated Parmesan
  cheese
¼ cup milk
1 large egg
2 garlic cloves, minced
½ tsp onion powder
½ tsp salt
¼ tsp black pepper

FOR THE SAUCE
1 cup barbecue sauce
¼ cup honey
¼ cup ketchup
1 tbsp soy sauce
1 tsp smoked paprika

1. **Prepare the meatballs.** In a large bowl, combine the ground beef, breadcrumbs, Parmesan cheese, milk, egg, minced garlic, onion powder, salt, and pepper. Mix until just combined, being careful not to overwork the meat. Form into small meatballs about 1 inch in diameter. Place the meatballs into the Crock-Pot.

2. **Make the sauce.** In a medium bowl, whisk together the barbecue sauce, honey, ketchup, soy sauce, and smoked paprika. In the Crock-Pot, pour the sauce over the meatballs, ensuring all are evenly coated.

3. **Cook.** Cover and cook on low for 4 to 6 hours or on high for 2 to 3 hours, until the meatballs are tender and cooked through to 160°F.

4. **Serve.** Before serving, stir the meatballs to coat them evenly in the sauce. Enjoy these easy, flavorful, and delicious meatballs with minimal cleanup!

Note: Feel free to substitute barbecue sauce with sugar-free barbecue sauce!

Layers of cheesy, saucy goodness—no oven needed!

HEALTHIER ONE-POT LASAGNA BOWL

When I was growing up, my mom made a *mean* lasagna—it was one of my absolute favorite dishes. But as I started focusing more on my health and fitness, I needed something that captured those comforting flavors without all the extra calories. This Healthier One-Pot Lasagna Bowl is the perfect solution. It's macro friendly and packed with lean protein, and it still delivers that cheesy, comforting goodness I loved as a kid.

Yield: Serves 4
Prep time: 10 minutes
Cook time: 20 minutes
Total time: 30 minutes

1lb ground turkey or (93% lean) ground beef
½ onion, diced
3 garlic cloves, minced
1 tsp Italian seasoning
½ tsp red pepper flakes (optional)
Salt and pepper, to taste
1 (14oz) can crushed tomatoes (no salt added)
2 cups low-sodium chicken broth
6oz whole wheat, chickpea, or regular lasagna noodles, broken into bite-size pieces
½ cup low-fat ricotta cheese
½ cup shredded part-skim mozzarella cheese
Cooking spray or olive oil
Fresh basil, for garnish

1. **Cook the meat.** Spray a large pot or Dutch oven with cooking spray or add a small amount of olive oil and place over medium heat. Add the ground turkey and cook until browned. Add the onion and garlic and sauté for 2 to 3 minutes, until softened. Stir in the Italian seasoning, red pepper flakes (if using), salt, and pepper.
2. **Add the sauce.** To the pot, pour in the crushed tomatoes and chicken broth. Bring to a simmer.
3. **Cook the noodles.** Directly into the pot, add the broken pieces of lasagna noodles. Stir well to coat the noodles in the sauce. Cover and cook for 10 to 12 minutes, stirring occasionally, until the noodles are tender and cooked through.
4. **Add the cheese.** Turn off the heat and stir in the low-fat ricotta cheese until well combined. Sprinkle the shredded mozzarella over top, cover, and allow the cheese to melt into the lasagna.
5. **Serve.** Spoon the lasagna into individual bowls and garnish with fresh basil. Enjoy a delicious, guilt-free meal that's big on flavor and easy on your macros!

Note: Whole wheat noodles provide a chewier texture while regular noodles will yield a more traditional lasagna experience. For a more robust flavor, increase the seasonings slightly or add a pinch of red pepper flakes, garlic powder, or Italian seasoning to taste.

FIRECRACKER SALMON BITES

Having an air fryer is a game changer, especially when you can make dishes like these Firecracker Salmon Bites in just 20 minutes. These bites are the perfect combo of sweet, spicy, and tangy, with crispy exteriors and tender centers. The firecracker sauce, made with honey, sriracha, light mayo, and sweet-chili sauce, adds bold flavors that take this recipe to the next level. And the best part? You can reserve some sauce to brush on after cooking for an extra kick.

Yield: Serves 4
Prep time: 10 minutes
Cook time: 7–9 minutes (Air Fryer) or 12–15 minutes (Oven)
Total time: 17–25 minutes

2 tbsp honey

2 tbsp sriracha

1 tbsp soy sauce (or tamari, for a gluten-free substitute)

1 tbsp rice vinegar

1 tbsp light mayo

1 tbsp sweet-chili sauce

1 tsp garlic powder

½ tsp onion powder

¼ tsp ground ginger

¼ tsp red pepper flakes (optional, for extra heat)

1lb salmon fillets, cut into bite-size pieces with the skin removed

2 green onions, chopped (optional, to garnish)

1. **Preheat the air fryer** to 385°F, or the oven to 400°F.
2. **Prepare the salmon.** In a large bowl, whisk together the honey, sriracha, soy sauce, rice vinegar, mayo, sweet-chili sauce, garlic powder, onion powder, ground ginger, and red pepper flakes (if using). Set aside half of the sauce to brush on after cooking. Toss the salmon bites in the remaining marinade, coating them well. Let the salmon marinate for 5 minutes.
3. **Cook the salmon.**
   Air fryer: Lightly spray an air-fryer basket with nonstick cooking oil. Arrange the salmon bites in a single layer in the basket and air-fry for 7 to 9 minutes until the salmon is crispy on the outside and cooked through to 125°F for medium rare, or to a maximum of 130°F.
   Oven: Line a baking sheet with parchment paper and arrange the salmon bites in a single layer. Bake for 12 to 15 minutes, or until the salmon is crispy on the outside and cooked through to 125°F for medium rare, or to a maximum of 130°F.
4. **Finish with the sauce.** Once the salmon bites are cooked, brush them with the reserved sauce for an extra layer of flavor.
5. **Serve.** Enjoy these sweet, spicy, and tangy salmon bites over rice, with veggies, or on their own as a delicious and quick meal!

Spicy, sweet, and irresistibly sticky!

HEALTHIER FISH & CHIPS

Getting enough fish in your diet is crucial for your health—think of all those omega-3s and lean protein! This Healthier Fish and Chips recipe is a fun and delicious way to get your fish intake, especially if you've got picky eaters at home. The crispy, golden fish pairs perfectly with the seasoned, air-fried chips, and when you dip it all in tartar sauce, the flavors and textures will have your taste buds in overdrive!

Yield: Serves 4
Prep time: 15 minutes
Cook time: 25–32 minutes
Total time: 40–47 minutes

FOR THE CHIPS

4 large Russet potatoes, cut into ½ in thick wedges
1 tbsp olive oil
½ tsp garlic powder
½ tsp paprika
½ tsp salt
¼ tsp black pepper

FOR THE FISH

½ cup all-purpose flour
½ cup panko breadcrumbs
¼ cup cornmeal
½ tsp garlic powder
½ tsp onion powder
½ tsp paprika
½ tsp salt
¼ tsp black pepper
1 large egg
1½lbs white-fish fillets (cod, haddock, etc.)
Olive oil spray

FOR THE TARTAR SAUCE

¼ cup light mayo
¼ cup plain nonfat Greek yogurt
1 tbsp sweet relish
1 tsp Dijon mustard
1 tsp lemon juice
1 tsp finely chopped capers
1 tsp chopped fresh dill
1 small garlic clove, minced
Salt and pepper, to taste

1. **Preheat the air fryer** to 385°F.
2. **Prepare the chips.** Bring a large pot of salted water to a boil over high heat, then add the potato wedges and cook for 3 to 4 minutes, until fork tender. Strain the potato wedges, shaking them as you do so to fluff the edges. Transfer to a large bowl and toss the potato wedges with the olive oil, garlic powder, paprika, salt, and pepper. To the bottom of the air-fryer basket, arrange the seasoned potato wedges in a single layer. Air-fry for 15 to 20 minutes, shaking halfway through, until golden and crispy. Set aside, keeping the air fryer preheated to 400°F for the fish.
3. **Bread the fish.** In a large shallow dish, combine the flour, breadcrumbs, cornmeal, garlic powder, onion powder, paprika, salt, and pepper. In a separate smaller dish, add the egg and whisk well. Dip each fish fillet first into the beaten egg, then into the breadcrumb mixture, pressing firmly to adhere. Lightly spray the fish fillets with olive oil.
4. **Cook the fish.** Place the breaded fish in a single layer in the air-fryer basket and cook for 10 to 12 minutes until crispy and golden.
5. **Make the tartar sauce.** While the fish cooks, in a small bowl, mix together the mayo, Greek yogurt, sweet relish, Dijon mustard, lemon juice, capers, dill, and minced garlic. Season with salt and pepper to taste.
6. **Serve.** Plate the crispy fish with the golden chips and a side of tartar sauce and enjoy a healthier version of this classic dish.

177

HEALTHIER RICE-CAKE S'MORES

S'mores are the ultimate camping treat, and my family and I have countless memories of enjoying them during bonfires at Huntington Beach, California. This version hits all the right notes—melty chocolate, gooey marshmallow, and satisfying crunchiness. The best part? You can enjoy that nostalgic, delicious s'mores flavor without worrying about overindulging. Whether you're reminiscing about past bonfires or just craving a quick sweet treat, these Healthier Rice-Cake S'mores are the perfect solution.

Yield: Makes 4

Prep time: 5 minutes

Cook time: 3–5 minutes (Air Fryer) or 5–7 minutes (Oven)

Total time: 8–12 minutes

4 rice cakes

4 squares of dark chocolate, broken into small pieces (70% cocoa or higher)

4–6 tbsp mini marshmallows

4 tbsp crushed graham crackers (optional, to garnish)

4 tbsp sugar-free chocolate syrup (optional, to garnish)

1. **Preheat the air fryer** to 400°F, or the oven to 425°F.
2. **Assemble the s'mores.** On each rice cake, evenly distribute the dark chocolate pieces. Top each with 1 to 2 tablespoons of the mini marshmallows.
3. **Cook the s'mores.**
   Air fry: Place the loaded rice cakes in an air-fryer basket and air-fry for 3 to 5 minutes until the marshmallows are slightly golden and gooey.
   Oven: On a baking sheet lined with parchment paper, place the loaded rice cakes. Bake for 5 to 7 minutes until the marshmallows are slightly golden and gooey.
4. **Garnish.** Top each with 1 tablespoon of the crushed graham crackers (if using) and 1 tablespoon of the sugar-free chocolate syrup (if using) and enjoy!

HEALTHIER MOIST CHOCOLATE CUPCAKES

You know how cupcakes always look better than they taste? Well, not this one. This healthier chocolate cupcake is everything you've been missing. It's moist, rich, and has the perfect balance of frosting, with a little surprise in the middle. Every bite is spot on—no more dry cake or too-sweet frosting.

Yield: Makes 12
Prep time: 15 minutes
Cook time: 22 minutes
Total time: 37 minutes

FOR THE FROSTING

¼ cup light cream cheese, softened to room temperature

2 tbsp unsalted butter, softened (optional)

½ tsp vanilla extract

⅛ tsp salt

½ cup powdered monk-fruit sweetener, or any powdered/confectioners' sugar alternative

¼ cup unsweetened cocoa powder

2–3 tsp Fairlife 2% milk

FOR THE CUPCAKES

1 cup cake flour (or all-purpose flour, if unavailable)

½ cup unsweetened cocoa powder

1 tsp baking powder

½ tsp baking soda

¼ tsp salt

¾ cup coconut sugar, or any sugar alternative

⅓ cup unsweetened applesauce

¼ cup plain or vanilla Greek yogurt

¼ cup light sour cream

2 tbsp unsalted butter, melted (optional)

⅓ cup Fairlife 2% milk (or milk of choice)

1 large egg

1 tsp vanilla extract

1. **Preheat the oven** to 325°F, and line a 12-cup muffin tin with cupcake liners.

2. **Make the frosting.** In a medium bowl, use an electric mixer to cream the cream cheese, butter (if using), vanilla, and salt until smooth and fluffy. Add the powdered monk-fruit and cocoa powder, beating until incorporated. Add 2 teaspoons of milk and beat on medium-high until thick and spreadable. Add an extra teaspoon of milk if needed. Set aside.

3. **Mix the dry ingredients.** In a large bowl, whisk together the flour, cocoa powder, baking powder, baking soda, and salt. Set aside.

4. **Mix the wet ingredients.** In a separate large bowl, use an electric mixer to combine the coconut sugar, applesauce, Greek yogurt, sour cream, butter (if using), milk, egg, and vanilla extract until smooth and creamy.

5. **Combine.** Gradually add the wet ingredients to the dry ingredients, gently folding until just combined (avoid overmixing).

6. **Fill the cupcake liners.** Fill each cupcake liner halfway with the batter. Add a dollop of frosting (about 1 teaspoon) to the center of each, then top with more batter to cover the frosting, ensuring each liner is about three-fourths full.

7. **Bake.** Bake for 20 to 22 minutes, or until a toothpick inserted into the edge (not the center with frosting) comes out clean. Let cool in the tin for 10 minutes before transferring to a wire rack to cool completely.

8. **Frost the cupcakes.** Once completely cooled, spread or pipe the remaining frosting evenly over the cupcakes.

Creamy, dreamy, berry goodness!

STRAWBERRY CHEESECAKE CUPS

These little macro-friendly bites of heaven will satisfy your cheesecake cravings in a fun and nutritious way. They're so easy to make that you can get kids involved too! With a creamy cheesecake filling and a fresh strawberry topping, these cups are the perfect sweet treat that won't derail your nutrition goals.

Yield: Makes 12
Prep time: 15 minutes
Cook time: 25 minutes
Chill time: 1 hour
Total time: 1 hour 40 minutes

FOR THE CRUST

1 cup crushed graham crackers (or almond flour, for a lower-carb option)
4 tbsp melted coconut oil
2 tbsp honey or maple syrup

FOR THE CHEESECAKE FILLING

1 cup fat-free cottage cheese
8oz light cream cheese, softened to room temperature
¼ cup powdered monk-fruit sweetener, or any powdered/confectioners' sugar alternative
1 scoop vanilla protein powder (optional)
1 tsp vanilla extract
1 large egg
2–3 tbsp unsweetened almond milk

FOR THE STRAWBERRY TOPPING

2 cups chopped strawberries
2 tbsp honey or maple syrup
1 tsp lemon juice

1. **Preheat the oven** to 350°F.
2. **Prepare the crust.** In a medium bowl, mix together the crushed graham crackers, melted coconut oil, and honey. To the bottom of a lined muffin tin or mini cheesecake molds, press the mixture evenly to create the crusts.
3. **Make the cheesecake filling.** In a blender or food processor, blend the cottage cheese until smooth. Add the softened cream cheese, powdered monk-fruit, protein powder (if using), vanilla extract, egg, and almond milk. Mix with a whisk or spatula until smooth.
4. **Assemble and bake.** Over each crust, spoon an equal amount of the cheesecake filling and smooth the tops with a spatula. Bake for 20 to 25 minutes, or until the edges are set but the centers are slightly jiggly.
5. **Make the strawberry topping.** While the cheesecake cups are baking, in a small bowl, combine the chopped strawberries, honey, and lemon juice. Stir well and set aside.
6. **Cool and chill.** Let the cheesecake cups cool to room temperature, then refrigerate for at least 1 hour or until fully set.
7. **Top and serve.** Once the cheesecake cups are chilled, carefully remove from the molds. Top each with the strawberry topping and serve.

OREO PROTEIN CHEESECAKE CUPS

Oreos were one of my favorite childhood snacks—my mom would always pack a few in my lunch box, so they hold a special place in my heart. These Oreo Protein Cheesecake Bites bring back all those nostalgic flavors along with a protein boost. By using Greek yogurt, light cream cheese, and protein powder, this version cuts down on sugar and fat while still delivering all the indulgence you crave.

Yield: Makes 12
Prep time: 10 minutes
Cook time: 25 minutes
Chill time: 1 hour
Total time: 1 hour 35 minutes

FOR THE CRUST
8 Oreo cookies (plus more
　for topping)
2 tbsp melted coconut oil

FOR THE CHEESECAKE FILLING
1 cup fat-free cottage cheese
8oz light cream cheese, softened
　to room temperature
¼ cup powdered monk-fruit
　sweetener, or any powdered/
　confectioners' sugar alternative
1 scoop vanilla protein powder
　(optional)
1 tsp vanilla extract
1 large egg
2–3 tbsp unsweetened almond milk

1. **Preheat the oven** to 350°F.
2. **Prepare the crust.** To a food processor or blender, add the Oreo cookies, and blend until the consistency resembles coarse crumbs. In a medium bowl, mix together the crushed Oreos and the melted coconut oil. To the bottom of a lined muffin tin or mini cheesecake molds, press the mixture into an even layer to form the crusts.
3. **Make the cheesecake filling.** To a blender or food processor, add the fat-free cottage cheese and blend until smooth. Add the cream cheese, powdered monk-fruit, protein powder (if using), vanilla extract, egg, and almond milk. Mix with a whisk, spatula, or electric mixer until smooth.
4. **Assemble and bake.** Over each crust, spoon an equal amount of the cheesecake filling and smooth the tops with a spatula. Bake for 20 to 25 minutes, or until the edges are set and the centers are slightly jiggly.
5. **Cool and chill.** Let the cheesecake cups cool to room temperature, then refrigerate for at least 1 hour or until fully set.
6. **Serve and top.** Once the cheesecake cups are chilled, carefully remove from the molds. If desired, sprinkle crushed Oreo crumbs on top for extra flavor. Enjoy!

HEALTHY OAT-FLOUR CARROT CAKE

Carrot cake is arguably one of the best cakes in existence. The natural sweetness and moisture from the carrots give the dessert an edge, while adding a boost of nutrients. The textures and flavors make this recipe a tasty treat that's hard to resist. This version made with oat flour is the best because it's not only delicious but it's also packed with fiber and whole grains, making it a satisfying and healthier option.

Yield: Serves 12
Prep time: 15 minutes
Cook time: 35 minutes
Total time: 50 minutes

FOR THE CAKE
2 cups oat flour
1½ tsp baking powder
½ tsp baking soda
½ tsp salt
2 tsp cinnamon
1 tsp nutmeg
1 tsp ginger
½ cup coconut sugar, or
   any sugar alternative
¼ cup unsweetened
   applesauce
½ cup plain full-fat
   Greek yogurt
⅓ cup honey or maple syrup
3 large eggs
1 tsp vanilla extract
2 cups grated carrots
½ cup crushed pineapple,
   drained
½ cup chopped walnuts or
   pecans (optional)

FOR THE CREAM-CHEESE FROSTING
8oz light cream cheese, softened
   to room temperature
¼ cup powdered monk-fruit sweetener,
   or any powdered/confectioners'
   sugar alternative
1 tsp vanilla extract
2 tbsp Greek yogurt

1. **Preheat the oven** to 350°F. Grease and flour a 9-inch round cake pan, or line with parchment paper.
2. **Mix the dry ingredients.** In a large bowl, whisk together the oat flour, baking powder, baking soda, salt, cinnamon, nutmeg, and ginger.
3. **Mix the wet ingredients.** In a separate large bowl, combine the coconut sugar, applesauce, Greek yogurt, honey, eggs, and vanilla extract. Beat until smooth.
4. **Combine.** Gradually add the wet ingredients to the dry ingredients, gently folding until just combined (avoid overmixing). Fold in the grated carrots, crushed pineapple, and the chopped nuts (if using).
5. **Bake.** Pour the batter into the prepared cake pan and smooth the top with a spatula. Bake for 30 to 35 minutes, or until a toothpick inserted into the center comes out clean. Allow the cake to cool completely in the pan.
6. **Make the frosting.** While the cake cools, in a medium bowl, beat together the cream cheese, powdered monk-fruit, vanilla extract, and Greek yogurt until smooth and creamy.
7. **Frost and serve.** Spread the cream-cheese frosting evenly over top of the cooled cake. Slice and enjoy this healthy, flavorful carrot cake that's perfect for satisfying your sweet tooth in a nutritious way!

HEALTHIER AIR-FRIED GLAZED DONUTS

Krispy Kreme might make the best donuts in the world, but Krispy KARIM makes the best nutritionally sound donuts in the world! This recipe gives you that same fluffy, melt-in-your-mouth texture with a sweet, irresistible glaze but with fewer calories—because they're air-fried. Perfectly light, perfectly sweet (just like you), and an awesome way to satisfy your donut cravings while sticking to your goals.

Yield: Makes 8
Prep time: 1 hour 20 minutes
Cook time: 4 minutes
Total time: 1 hour 24 minutes

FOR THE DONUTS
1¾ cups all-purpose flour
2 tbsp sugar
½ tsp salt
½ tsp cinnamon (optional)
1 tsp instant yeast
½ cup warm milk (Fairlife 2%, for a healthier option)
2 tbsp unsweetened applesauce
1 large egg (at room temperature)
½ tsp vanilla extract
Avocado oil spray

FOR THE GLAZE
½ cup powdered monk-fruit sweetener, or any powdered/confectioners' sugar alternative
1 tbsp unsweetened almond milk
½ tsp vanilla extract

1. **Prepare the dough.** In a large bowl, whisk together the flour, sugar, salt, cinnamon (if using), and yeast. In a separate medium bowl, whisk together the warm milk, applesauce, egg, and vanilla extract. Pour the wet ingredients into the dry ingredients and mix until a dough forms.
2. **Knead and rise.** On a lightly floured surface, knead the dough for about 5 minutes, until smooth and elastic. Spray a medium bowl with avocado oil, transfer the dough to the bowl, cover, and let rise for about 1 hour, or until it doubles in size.
3. **Shape the donuts.** On a clean, floured surface, roll out the dough to about ½-inch thickness. Using a donut cutter or 2 round cutters (a 3-inch cutter for the donut itself and a 1-inch cutter for the hole), cut out the donuts. Place the donuts on a parchment-lined baking sheet and let rise for another 10 to 15 minutes.
4. **Air-fry the donuts.** Preheat the air fryer to 350°F. Lightly spray the donuts with avocado oil. Place the donuts in a single layer in the air-fryer basket and cook for 4 minutes, without flipping, until golden brown and fluffy. Repeat with any remaining donuts and donut holes.
5. **Make the glaze.** While the donuts are cooking, in a small bowl, use an electric mixer or whisk to combine the powdered monk-fruit sweetener, almond milk, and vanilla extract until smooth and slightly thickened.
6. **Glaze the donuts.** Dip the warm donuts into the glaze, coating the tops evenly. Allow any excess to drip off before transferring the donuts to a wire rack to set.
7. **Serve.** Enjoy these light, fluffy, and perfectly sweetened donuts warm.

Note: If the dough is sticky, sprinkle additional flour as needed while shaping and rolling.

Sweet, protein-packed, and guilt-free!

PROTEIN COPYCAT CINNABON ROLLS

When I was a kid living in Saudi Arabia, I was obsessed with the smell of Cinnabon rolls during family shopping trips. That warm, sugary aroma filled the mall, and I couldn't resist. These healthier protein cinnamon rolls bring back all those memories but with a twist. They're fluffy, loaded with flavor, and have that gooey cinnamon-sugar filling, just like the original. The best part? They're packed with extra protein!

Yield: Makes 8
Prep time: 1 hour 20 minutes
Cook time: 10 minutes
Total time: 1 hour 30 minutes

FOR THE DOUGH

½ cup + 2 tbsp warm water or
   Fairlife 2% milk (120°F–130°F)
1 tbsp sugar
1 (0.25oz) fast-acting yeast packet
2 cups all-purpose flour
½ cup vanilla protein powder
1 tbsp unsalted butter, melted

FOR THE FILLING

¼ cup monk-fruit brown sugar
2 tbsp cinnamon
2 tbsp melted butter or coconut oil

FOR THE FROSTING

2oz light cream cheese, softened
2 tbsp unsalted butter, softened
2–3 tsp milk (start with 2 tsp and add
   more as needed)
½ tsp vanilla extract
⅛ tsp salt
½ cup powdered sugar or monk-fruit
   confectioner sugar

1. **Prepare the dough.** In a medium bowl, combine the warm water with the sugar and yeast. Whisk until dissolved and let sit for 10 minutes. Gradually stir in the flour, protein powder, and melted butter until combined, adding more flour if needed. The dough should be slightly sticky.

2. **Knead and rise.** On a lightly floured surface, knead the dough for about 5 minutes, until smooth and elastic. Place the dough in a greased bowl, cover with a towel, and let it rise in a warm place for 10 to 20 minutes, or until doubled in size. To create a warm environment, you can place the bowl in a microwave with a bowl of boiled water.

3. **Make the filling.** In a small bowl, mix together the monk-fruit brown sugar, cinnamon, and melted butter until it forms a spreadable paste.

4. **Roll and fill.** On a lightly floured surface, roll out the dough into a 14×8-inch rectangle. Spread the cinnamon-sugar filling evenly over the dough. Roll the dough tightly into a log and seal the edges. Using a serrated knife, slice the log into eight 1.5-inch rolls.

5. **Bake.** Preheat the oven to 325°F. Grease a 9x13-inch baking dish. Place the rolls in the dish, cover, and let rise while the oven preheats. Bake for 8 to 10 minutes, checking frequently toward the end to avoid overbaking. The rolls will continue to bake slightly in the hot pan after removal.

6. **Make the frosting.** While the rolls are baking, prepare the frosting. Using a hand mixer, blend the cream cheese, softened butter, milk, vanilla, and salt. Gradually add the powdered sugar and mix until smooth.

7. **Frost and serve.** Spread the frosting over the warm rolls and enjoy!

JAPANESE SOUFFLÉ PANCAKES

Growing up, I was never the biggest sweets guy, but the first time I tried Japanese soufflé pancakes, I teleported to a different world. They're fluffy, airy, and have this incredible melt-in-your-mouth texture that's light yet satisfying. The subtle sweetness and the vanilla-infused flavor make them irresistible. This version incorporates vanilla protein Greek yogurt, giving them a little extra boost of flavor and nutrition.

Yield: Makes 12
Prep time: 15 minutes
Cook time: 30 minutes
Total time: 45 minutes

4 large eggs, whites and
   yolks separated
Pinch of salt
2 tbsp monk-fruit sweetener,
   or any sugar alternative
½ cup vanilla protein
   Greek yogurt
¼ cup all-purpose flour
1 tsp baking powder
1 tsp vanilla extract
2 tbsp Fairlife 2% milk
   (or milk of choice)
Fresh berries, for topping

1. **Prepare the egg whites.** For optimal results, chill the bowl and beaters in the freezer for a few minutes before starting this step. In a large, clean, dry stainless-steel bowl, add the egg whites and pinch of salt. Using an electric mixer (recommended), whisk until stiff peaks form. Gradually add the monk fruit sweetener while whisking to stabilize the meringue.

2. **Mix the egg yolks.** In a separate large bowl, whisk together the egg yolks, Greek yogurt, flour, baking powder, vanilla extract, and milk until smooth and well combined.

3. **Combine.** Working in batches, gently fold the egg whites into the egg-yolk mixture, being careful not to deflate the mixture. Take your time to maintain its light and airy texture.

4. **Cook the pancakes.** Heat a large nonstick skillet over low heat and lightly spray with avocado oil. Spoon 3 to 4 large spoonfuls of batter into the skillet to form a thick pancake and repeat for a second pancake. Cover with a lid and cook for 3 to 4 minutes on each side until golden brown and cooked through. Repeat for the rest of the batter, cooking 2 pancakes at a time and greasing the pan lightly after each batch to prevent sticking.

5. **Serve.** Serve the pancakes warm with your favorite toppings, such as fresh berries, a dollop of Greek yogurt, or a drizzle of syrup. Enjoy these light, fluffy pancakes that are well worth the effort!

Fluffy, airy stacks of heaven!

Lotus Biscoff

Oreo

Peanut Butter

HEALTHIER MILKSHAKES
OREO, PEANUT BUTTER & LOTUS BISCOFF

When I was younger, I was obsessed with Baskin-Robbins's milkshakes. I'd always beg my dad to stop and get me one, whether it was Oreo, peanut butter, or something new like Lotus Biscoff. These healthier versions bring back those childhood memories but with a nutritious twist. They're creamy and rich, and they have the perfect milkshake consistency, plus they're packed with protein, so they taste incredible while keeping you on track.

Yield: 2 servings
Prep time: 5 minutes
Cook time: 0 minutes
Total time: 5 minutes

OREO MILKSHAKE

1 cup Fairlife 2% milk
60g vanilla protein powder
　(whey preferred)
4 Oreo cookies (or a sugar-free
　alternative)
¼ cup plain nonfat Greek yogurt
½ cup ice
¼ tsp xanthan gum (optional)
2 tbsp whipped topping (optional,
　for garnish)

1. Blend all ingredients in a high-speed blender until smooth. If the mixture is too thin, add an additional ¼ teaspoon of xanthan gum or more ice for a thicker texture.
2. Pour into a glass and garnish with whipped topping (if using), crushed Oreos, or both for extra indulgence. Serve immediately.

PEANUT BUTTER MILKSHAKE

1 cup Fairlife 2% milk
60g vanilla protein powder
　(whey preferred)
2 tbsp natural peanut butter
¼ cup plain nonfat Greek yogurt
½ cup ice
¼ tsp xanthan gum
2 tbsp whipped topping (optional,
　for garnish)

1. Blend all ingredients in a high-speed blender until smooth. For a thicker milkshake consistency, add an extra ¼ teaspoon of xanthan gum or more ice.
2. Pour into a glass and garnish with whipped topping (if using) and a drizzle of peanut butter, if desired. Serve immediately.

LOTUS BISCOFF MILKSHAKE

1 cup Fairlife 2% milk
60g vanilla protein powder
　(whey preferred)
2 tbsp Lotus Biscoff spread
¼ cup plain nonfat Greek yogurt
½ cup ice
¼ tsp xanthan gum
2 tbsp whipped topping (optional,
　for garnish)

1. Blend all ingredients in a high-speed blender until smooth and creamy. Add an extra ¼ teaspoon of xanthan gum or more ice if a thicker consistency is desired.
2. Pour into a glass and garnish with whipped topping (if using) and crushed Biscoff cookies, if desired. Serve immediately.

ACKNOWLEDGMENTS

This cookbook would not have been possible without the support and hard work of an incredible team. To Adam, our talented food stylist, your creativity brought these dishes to life in a way that made them jump off the page. Ivan, your eye for detail and passion behind the camera captured the heart of every recipe. And Joanna, thank you for keeping everything running smoothly and making sure every detail was just right—I'm so grateful for your coordination and dedication.

To my parents, your sacrifices and unwavering support have shaped me into who I am today. You made the decision to live apart for over a decade, leaving everything behind to give our family a better future. Moving to the US at 12 was a new beginning for me, and I carry the strength and resilience you taught me in everything I do. You taught me perseverance and the importance of chasing after what truly matters. I owe this journey to you. This cookbook wouldn't exist without the opportunities you fought to create.

To my junior-year honors English teacher, Mr. Hallstrom, you were one of the first people to believe in me before I even believed in myself. Your encouragement to express myself and embrace my creativity has stuck with me through the years. It's amazing how much impact a single teacher can have on someone's life, and I'm forever grateful for the role you played in mine.

Lastly, to my incredible community of over six million people, thank you. You've believed in me, supported me, and trusted me to inspire you in your kitchens since 2020. Your support has given me the platform to share my passion, and it's because of you that I can bring this cookbook to life. This book is as much yours as it is mine. From the bottom of my heart, thank you.

INDEX

4-Ingredient Protein Everything Bagel, 28–29

A

Air-Fried Chips, 89
Air-Fryer Mozzarella Sticks, 52–53
appliances, 15
author's story, 9

B

baked goods. *See* breads and baked goods
Barbecue Chicken Pizza with Lavash Bread, 118–119
beef. *See also* burgers
    Big Mac Salad, 90–91
    Big Mac Smash Tacos, 128–129
    Copycat McDonald's Big Mac, 144–145
    Copycat McDonald's Cheeseburger, 140–141
    Copycat Sausage & Egg McMuffin, 30–31
    Copycat Whopper, 146–147
    Crispy, Baked Beef Tacos, 126–127
    Grilled Kofta Pita Pockets with Tahini-Yogurt Sauce, 108

    Healthier Copycat In-N-Out Double-Double, 150–151
    Healthier Copycat Juicy Lucy Burger, 148–149
    Healthier One-Pot Lasagna Bowl, 172–173
    Healthier Steakhouse Burger, 152–153
    High-Protein, Low-Calorie Loaded Nachos, 56–57
    Honey-Barbecue Slow-Cooker Meatballs, 170–171
    Korean Beef Wraps, 106–107
    Loaded Bacon Cheddar Fries, 46–47
    Mexican-Inspired Loaded Baked Potato, 76–77
Big Mac Salad, 90–91
Big Mac Smash Tacos, 128–129
breads and baked goods
    4-Ingredient Protein Everything Bagel, 28–29
    Healthier Air-Fried Glazed Donuts, 192–193
    Healthier Moist Chocolate Cupcakes, 182–183
    Healthy Oat-Flower Carrot Cake, 188–189
    High-Protein, Low-Calorie Garlic Cheese Bread, 44–45
    Japanese Soufflé Pancakes, 196–197

Keto Pizza Dough, 112–113

breakfast

4-Ingredient Protein Everything Bagel, 28–29

Chocolate-Chip Baked Oats, 38–39

Copycat McGriddle, 32–33

Copycat Philz Green Chile Burrito, 36–37

Copycat Sausage & Egg McMuffin, 30–31

Copycat Starbucks Bacon & Gruyère Egg Bites, 24–25

Copycat Starbucks Kale & Mushroom Egg Bites, 22–23

Copycat Starbucks Spinach, Feta & Egg White Wrap, 34–35

Hash Browns, 26–27

Macro-Friendly Cinnamon-Roll Pancakes, 40–41

Buffalo chicken

Buffalo Wings, 67

Crispy Buffalo-Chicken Tacos, 124–125

Buffalo Wild Wings copycats

Buffalo Wings, 67

Honey-Barbecue Wings, 68

Buffalo Wings, 67

Burger King copycats

Copycat Whopper, 146–147

Crispy Onion rings, 78–79

burgers. *See also* beef

Copycat McDonald's Big Mac, 144–145

Copycat McDonald's Cheeseburger, 140–141

Copycat Spicy McChicken Sandwich, 138–139

Copycat Whopper, 146–147

Healthier Copycat In-N-Out Double-Double, 150–151

Healthier Copycat Juicy Lucy Burger, 148–149

Healthier Steakhouse Burger, 152–153

Turkey Burger with Lemon Aioli, 136–137

C

Chick-Fil-A copycats

Copycat Chick-Fil-A Southwest Salad with Creamy Salsa Dressing, 86–88

Healthier Copycat Chick-Fil-A Chicken Sandwich, 102

chicken

Barbecue Chicken Pizza with Lavash Bread, 118–119

Chicken Nuggets, 60

Chicken Shawarma Wrap, 103

Chicken Tenders, 62

Copycat Del Taco Chicken Soft Tacos, 122–123

Copycat Panda Express Teriyaki Chicken, 162

Copycat Spicy McChicken Sandwich, 138–139

Crispy Buffalo-Chicken Tacos, 124–125

Healthier Bang Bang Chicken Bites, 61

Healthier Chicken Parmesan, 156–157

Healthier Copycat Chick-Fil-A Chicken Sandwich, 102

Healthier Copycat Panda Express Orange Chicken, 160–161

Healthier Copycat Popeyes Chicken Sandwich, 98–99

Honey-Chipotle Chicken Rice Bowl, 166–167

Low-Calorie Copycat Chicken Snack Wrap, 100–101

One-Pan Korean Fried Chicken, 164–165

One-Pan Lemon-Chicken Orzo Pasta, 163

Chicken Nuggets, 60

Chicken Shawarma Wrap, 103

Chicken Tenders, 62

chicken wings

Buffalo Wings, 67

Garlic-Parmesan Wings, 66

Honey-Barbecue Wings, 68

Lemon-Pepper Wings, 64–65

Chinese Takeout Fried Rice, 92–93

Chipotle-Shrimp Tacos with Creamy Slaw, 130–131

Chocolate-Chip Baked Oats, 38–39

Cinnabon copycat, Protein Copycat Cinnabon Rolls, 194–195

Copycat Chick-Fil-A Southwest Salad with Creamy Salsa Dressing, 86–88

Copycat Del Taco Chicken Soft Tacos, 122–123

Copycat McDonald's Big Mac, 144–145

Copycat McDonald's Cheeseburger, 140–141

Copycat McGriddle, 32–33

Copycat Panda Express Teriyaki Chicken, 162

Copycat Philz Green Chile Burrito, 36–37

Copycat Sausage & Egg McMuffin, 30–31

Copycat Spicy McChicken Sandwich, 138–139

Copycat Starbucks Bacon & Gruyère Egg Bites, 24–25

Copycat Starbucks Kale & Mushroom Egg Bites, 22–23

Copycat Starbucks Spinach, Feta & Egg White Wrap, 34–35

Copycat Whopper, 146–147

Crispy Buffalo-Chicken Tacos, 124–125

Crispy Onion rings, 78–79

Crispy Smashed Potato Salad, 84–85

Crispy, Baked Beef Tacos, 126–127

D

Del Taco copycat, Copycat Del Taco Chicken Soft Tacos, 122–123

desserts and sweets. *See* sweets

E

Easy Healthier Cheese Pizza, 116–117

eggs

Copycat Starbucks Bacon & Gruyère Egg Bites, 24–25

Copycat Starbucks Kale & Mushroom Egg Bites, 22–23

Copycat Starbucks Spinach, Feta & Egg White Wrap, 34–35

equipment, 15

F

Firecracker Salmon Bites, 174–175

fish and seafood

Chipotle-Shrimp Tacos with Creamy Slaw, 130–131

Firecracker Salmon Bites, 174–175

Healthier Baja Fish Tacos, 132–133

Healthier Fish & Chips, 176–177

Popcorn Shrimp, 58–59

freezing sauces, 19

G

Garlic-Parmesan Wings, 66

Grilled Kofta Pita Pockets with Tahini-Yogurt Sauce, 108

H

handhelds. *See also* sandwiches and wraps

Hash Browns, 26–27

Healthier Air-Fried Glazed Donuts, 192–193

Healthier Baja Fish Tacos, 132–133

Healthier Bang Bang Chicken Bites, 61

Healthier Caesar Salad with Yogurt Dressing, 82–83

Healthier Chicken Parmesan, 156–157

Healthier Copycat Chick-Fil-A Chicken Sandwich, 102

Healthier Copycat In-N-Out Double-Double, 150–151

Healthier Copycat Juicy Lucy Burger, 148–149

Healthier Copycat Panda Express Orange Chicken, 160–161

Healthier Copycat Popeyes Chicken Sandwich, 98–99

Healthier Fish & Chips, 176–177

Healthier Milkshakes, 198–199

Healthier Moist Chocolate Cupcakes, 182–183

Healthier One-Pot Lasagna Bowl, 172–173

Healthier Pizza Toasties, 114–115

Healthier Rice-Cake S'Mores, 180–181

Healthier Steakhouse Burger, 152–153

Healthy Oat-Flower Carrot Cake, 188–189

High-Protein Mac 'N' Cheese, 168–169

High-Protein, Low-Calorie Garlic Cheese Bread, 44–45

High-Protein, Low-Calorie Grinder Sandwiches, 96–97

High-Protein, Low-Calorie Loaded Nachos, 56–57

Homemade Fast-Food Fries, 74–75

Honey-Barbecue Slow-Cooker Meatballs, 170–171

Honey-Barbecue Wings, 68

Honey-Chipotle Chicken Rice Bowl, 166–167

I

In-N-Out copycat, Healthier Copycat In-N-Out Double-Double, 150–151

J

Japanese Soufflé Pancakes, 196–197

Juicy Lucy copycat, Healthier Copycat Juicy Lucy Burger, 148–149

K

Keto Pizza Dough, 112–113

knives, 15

Korean Beef Wraps, 106–107

L

Lemon-Pepper Wings, 64–65

Loaded Bacon Cheddar Fries, 46–47

Low-Calorie Copycat Chicken Snack Wrap, 100–101

Low-Calorie Poutine, 48–49

Low-Calorie Tortilla Chips, 54–55

Lower-Calorie California Burrito, 104–105

M

Macro-Friendly Cinnamon-Roll Pancakes, 40–41

macro-friendly cooking, 10

main dishes

    Copycat Panda Express Teriyaki Chicken, 162

    Firecracker Salmon Bites, 174–175

    Healthier Chicken Parmesan, 156–157

    Healthier Copycat Panda Express Orange Chicken, 160–161

    Healthier Fish & Chips, 176–177

    Healthier One-Pot Lasagna Bowl, 172–173

    High-Protein Mac 'N' Cheese, 168–169

    Honey-Barbecue Slow-Cooker Meatballs, 170–171

    Honey-Chipotle Chicken Rice Bowl, 166–167

    One-Pan Korean Fried Chicken, 164–165

    One-Pan Lemon-Chicken Orzo Pasta, 163

McDonald's copycats

    Big Mac Salad, 90–91

    Big Mac Smash Tacos, 128–129

    Copycat McDonald's Big Mac, 144–145

    Copycat McDonald's Cheeseburger, 140–141

    Copycat McGriddle, 32–33

    Copycat Sausage & Egg McMuffin, 30–31

    Copycat Spicy McChicken Sandwich, 138–139

    Hash Browns, 26–27

meal plans, 16

measuring tools, 15

Mexican-Inspired Loaded Baked Potato, 76–77

N

nonstick skillets, 15

O

oils, 15

One-Pan Korean Fried Chicken, 164–165

One-Pan Lemon-Chicken Orzo Pasta, 163

Oreo Protein Cheesecake Cups, 186–187

P

Panda Express copycats

Copycat Panda Express Teriyaki Chicken, 162

Healthier Copycat Panda Express Orange Chicken, 160–161

pans, 15

pantry staples, 14

Philz Coffee copycat, Copycat Philz Green Chile Burrito, 36–37

pizza

Barbecue Chicken Pizza with Lavash Bread, 118–119

Easy Healthier Cheese Pizza, 116–117

Healthier Pizza Toasties, 114–115

Keto Pizza Dough, 112–113

Popcorn Shrimp, 58–59

Popeyes copycat, Healthier Copycat Popeyes Chicken Sandwich, 98–99

Protein Copycat Cinnabon Rolls, 194–195

proteins, 15

S

salads. *See* sides and salads

sandwiches and wraps

Chicken Shawarma Wrap, 103

Grilled Kofta Pita Pockets with Tahini-Yogurt Sauce, 108

Healthier Copycat Chick-Fil-A Chicken Sandwich, 102

Healthier Copycat Popeyes Chicken Sandwich, 98–99

High-Protein, Low-Calorie Grinder Sandwiches, 96–97

Korean Beef Wraps, 106–107

Low-Calorie Copycat Chicken Snack Wrap, 100–101

Lower-Calorie California Burrito, 104–105

Turkey Pesto Wrap, 109

sauces

Cilantro Avocado Sauce, 19

Creamy Chipotle Sauce, 19

Garlicky White Sauce, 19

Honey-Garlic Sauce, 18

Spicy Bang Bang Sauce, 18

seasonings, 15

sides and salads

Air-Fried Chips, 89

Big Mac Salad, 90–91

Chinese Takeout Fried Rice, 92–93

Copycat Chick-Fil-A Southwest Salad with Creamy Salsa Dressing, 86–88

Crispy Onion rings, 78–79

Crispy Smashed Potato Salad, 84–85

Healthier Caesar Salad with Yogurt Dressing, 82–83

High-Protein, Low-Calorie Grinder Sandwiches, 96–97

Homemade Fast-Food Fries, 74–75

Mexican-Inspired Loaded Baked Potato, 76–77

Sweet Potato Fries with Low-Calorie Chipotle Aioli, 72–73

Starbucks copycats

Copycat Starbucks Bacon & Gruyère Egg Bites, 24–25

Copycat Starbucks Kale & Mushroom Egg Bites, 22–23

Copycat Starbucks Spinach, Feta & Egg White Wrap, 34–35

starters

Air-Fryer Mozzarella Sticks, 52–53

Buffalo Wings, 67

Chicken Nuggets, 60

Chicken Tenders, 62

Garlic-Parmesan Wings, 66

Healthier Bang Bang Chicken Bites, 61

High-Protein, Low-Calorie Garlic Cheese Bread, 44–45

High-Protein, Low-Calorie Loaded Nachos, 56–57

Honey-Barbecue Wings, 68

Lemon-Pepper Wings, 64–65

Loaded Bacon Cheddar Fries, 46–47

Low-Calorie Poutine, 48–49

Low-Calorie Tortilla Chips, 54–55

Popcorn Shrimp, 58–59

storing sauces, 19

Strawberry Cheesecake Cups, 184–185

Sweet Potato Fries with Low-Calorie Chipotle Aioli, 72–73

sweets

Healthier Air-Fried Glazed Donuts, 192–193

Healthier Milkshakes, 198–199

Healthier Moist Chocolate Cupcakes, 182–183

Healthier Rice-Cake S'Mores, 180–181

Healthy Oat-Flower Carrot Cake, 188–189

Japanese Soufflé Pancakes, 196–197

Lotus Biscoff Milkshake, 198–199

Oreo Milkshake, 198–199

Oreo Protein Cheesecake Cups, 186–187

Peanut Butter Milkshake, 198–199

Protein Copycat Cinnabon Rolls, 194–195

Strawberry Cheesecake Cups, 184–185

T

tacos

Big Mac Smash Tacos, 128–129

Chipotle-Shrimp Tacos with Creamy Slaw, 130–131

Copycat Del Taco Chicken Soft Tacos, 122–123

Crispy Buffalo-Chicken Tacos, 124–125

Crispy, Baked Beef Tacos, 126–127

Healthier Baja Fish Tacos, 132–133

thermometer, 15

tools, 15

treats. *See* sweets

Turkey Burger with Lemon Aioli, 136–137

Turkey Pesto Wrap, 109

W–Z

Wingstop copycat, Lemon-Pepper Wings, 64–65

wraps. *See* sandwiches and wraps

ABOUT THE AUTHOR

Karim Saad is a passionate home cook and health enthusiast. After years of struggling with his weight, he was able to find the perfect balance between indulging in fast food and maintaining a healthy lifestyle. Karim embarked on a weight-loss journey where he lost 40 pounds by recreating his favorite fast-food recipes and restaurant dishes with a nutritious twist. His life's mission is to inspire others to enjoy delicious, guilt-free fast-food alternatives without compromising on taste or health and break down the stigma that "eating healthy is boring." He has built a community of over 6 million followers across social media and strives to inspire others with simple nutritious recipes.

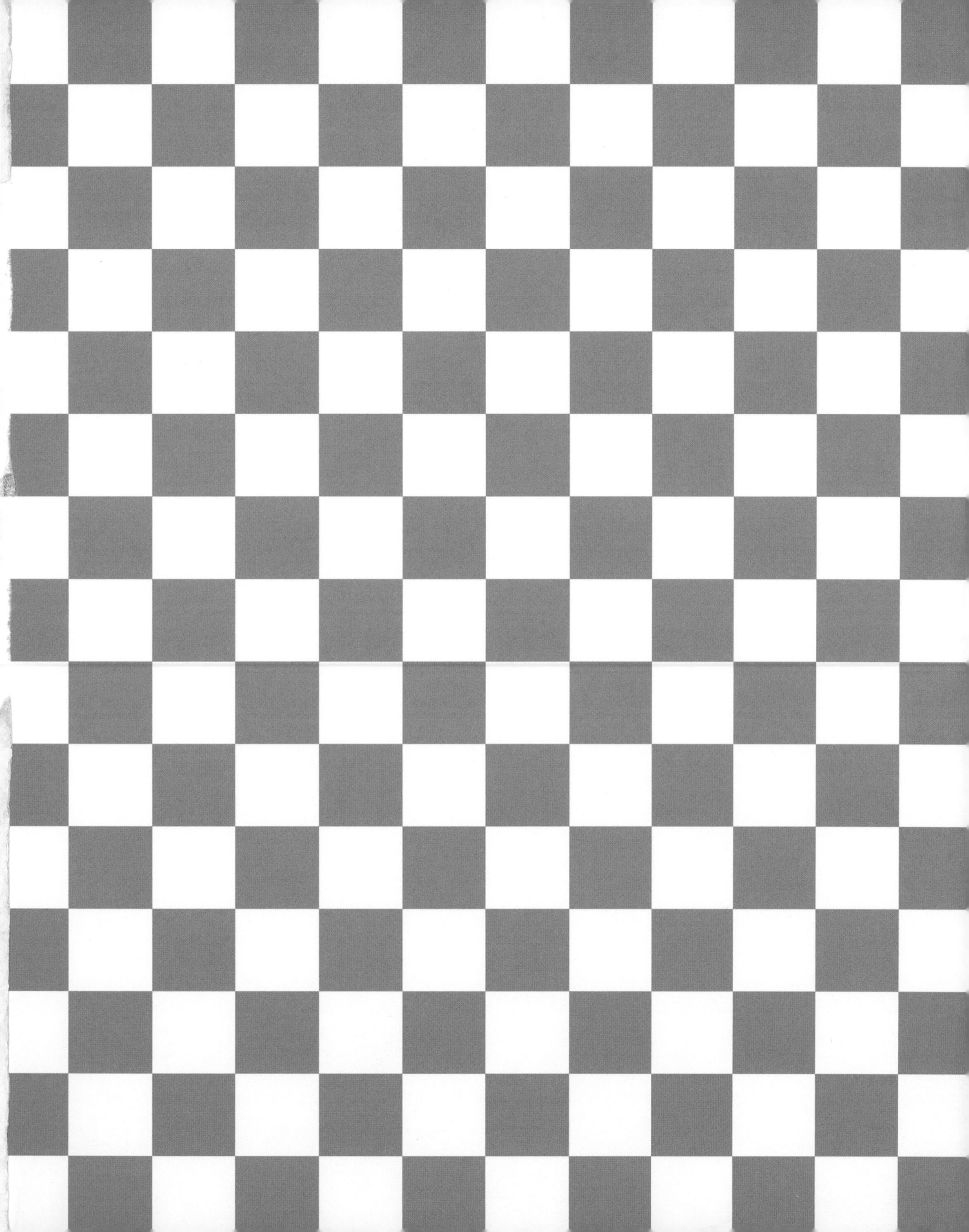